POLITICAL ECOLOGY

POLITICAL ECOLOGY

Beyond Environmentalism

DIMITRIOS I. ROUSSOPOULOS

BLACK ROSE BOOKS

Montréal/New York

London

BLACK ROSE BOOKS No. W189
Hardcover ISBN 1-895431-81-6
Paperback ISBN 1-895431-80-8

Library of Congress No. 93-072749

Canadian Cataloguing in Publication Data

Roussopoulos, Dimitrios I.,
Political ecology: beyond environmentalism

Includes bibliographical references.
ISBN: 1-895431-81-6 (bound)
ISBN: 1-895431-80-8 (pbk.)

1. Human ecology — Political aspects. 2. Environmental protection — Citizen participation. 3. Environmental policy. 4. Green movement. I. Title.

GF80.R69 1993   363.7'05613   C93 - 090489 - 3

Book design and layout: April Hubert
Relief used on cover:
Democracy placing a wreath on the people of Athens, celebrating self-government. The releif, found in the Agora, was to remind the citizens of their freedom.

BLACK ROSE BOOKS
C.P. 1258
Succ. Place du Parc
Montréal, Québec
H2W 2R3 Canada

BLACK ROSE BOOKS
340 Nagel Drive
Cheektowaga, New York
14225 USA

Mailing Address

Printed in Canada

A publication of the Institute of Policy Alternatives of Montréal

Table of contents

Introduction

The first State pollution agency was established some 125 years ago, and it is now over a century since the first international environment agreement between nation-States was signed. In the 20 years before the publication of the Brundtland Report, more than 130 nation-States created environmental agencies; more than 180 international agreements were signed; and the United Nations created a new global environmental programme. Yet the results of this flurry of activity ostensibly intended to reverse the advance of ecological destruction are far from satisfactory.

The first section of this book, *Towards the State Management of the Environment*, traces the various efforts on the part of governments to elaborate State environmental policies to deal with the ecological crisis.

Section two, *The Ecological Crisis and the Response of Citizens to the Plight of the Earth*, begins with a survey of main elements of the ecological crisis, providing an overview of the deteriorating state of the environment, and underscoring the failure of State action to date to solve global environmental problems.

This section goes on to discuss the range of efforts undertaken by people in various countries to deal with environmental problems. It examines some of the principal concepts within environmentalism such as preservationism and conservationism, exploring the genesis and impact of these ideas and the nature of the groups which advocated them. It goes on to glance very briefly at other more radical responses to the environmental crisis including environmental populism, deep ecology, bio-regionalism and eco-feminism.

Section three, *Political Ecology and Social Ecology*, offers a discussion of the Greens and of the formation of Green political parties intended to illuminate the differences between ecologists and environmentalists. It also presents a case study of the Greens in France. This exploration of Green political history sets the context for a discussion of what are arguably the most significant historical responses to the environmental crisis, namely eco-socialism, green social democracy, eco-Marxism and, finally, social ecology.

The social and political implications of the programmes and strategies advanced by environmentalists and ecologists must be analysed quite apart from how laudable or feasible the goals of these groups may be. Are Green movements the model of a new politics, transcending both the old social democratic and Leninist vanguard political parties? Are environmentalists who avoid attacking and attempting to transform the institutions of power doomed to ineffectuality? Given the prevailing historical, economic, political and military trends which point towards ever greater global integration, how can decentralisation and democratic self-reliance be achieved; how can we create a confederation of libertarian eco-communities? These and other timely questions are raised in this text in an effort to shed light on diverse perspectives and enrich the debate on the prospects of building an ecological society.

Acknowledgements

The editorial work of my friend and colleague Andrea Levy is most appreciated. I would also like to thank Linda Barton for her work on one of the sections of the book. The word-processing and layout was admirably done by April Hubert to whom I am most grateful.

Towards
The State Management of
the Environment

SECTION ONE

Towards
The State Management
Of The Environment

It is by now commonly acknowledged that we are in the midst of an increasingly acute ecological crisis. We are in fact, jeopardizing the very survival of the human species, as well as other life forms on our planet. How we are to understand this crisis and embark on an effective course for change before it is too late remain open questions.

Human misuse of the environment is not a new phenomenon. As many as 3700 years ago, for example, Sumerian cities were deserted by their populations because the irrigated soil which produced the world's first agricultural surpluses became saline and waterlogged. Plato is recorded complaining of the deforestation of the hills of Attica which were being deforested as a result of trees being cut for fuel and because of soil erosion due to overgrazing. There were warnings about crop failure and soil erosion as a result of animal husbandry practices as far back as first century Rome. Shipbuilding by Byzantines, Venetians and Genoans cut away large tracks of coastal forest around the Mediterranean. Coal-burning caused so much air pollution in the 1660's that London commentators complained bitterly. There was speculation about acid rain in the 1600's, which was scientifically confirmed by the 1850's. The current population debate dates back to work by Sir William Petty in the mid 1660's, to be picked up again by Thomas Malthus some one hundred and fifty years later.

It was only with the capitalist industrial revolution, however, that the endemic ravage of nature began, and with it a measure of public concern. The theory that industrialism is unsustainable because of its excessive strains on the natural environment was put forward over a century ago, in the works of the geographer and anarchist philosopher Peter Kropotkin.[1] And in the nineteenth century, too, wilderness protectionists and conservationists began speaking out in several countries. As the natural sciences revealed more of the workings of nature and of the deleterious effects of the relentless subjugation of the natural world, alarm grew on the part of a small informed public. This interplay of accumulating scientific knowledge and informed opinion developed steadily until after the Second World War, when awareness of environmental problems began to extend to the broader public. By the 1960's, the environment became the focal point of a social movement.

The first comprehensive air pollution law in the world was passed in Britain in 1863. The law also brought into being the first pollution control agency. More than one hundred years later, only 12 such agencies had been created. Today such agencies exist in the vast majority of nation-States. In 1886, the first international environmental agreement was signed, today there are over 250 agreements most of them concluded since the 1960's. Since the 1972 United Nations conference on the environment in Stockholm, almost all important international bodies, from the Organisation for Economic Cooperation and Development to the World Bank, have adopted environmental protection programmes. Since the Stockholm conference, some 10,000 new environmental groups have come into being adding to some 15,000 such groups which had been formed prior to the conference.

Before The Second World War

Environmental awareness grew gradually among wider segments of the public as scientific evidence accumulated and the immediate effects of pollution, the loss of woodlands, and other forms of environmental degradation became clearly visible.

As we have noted, insight into how nature functions and into the relationships between all life forms goes back centuries. Just before he set sail for the Americas in 1799, the naturalist Alexander von Humboldt wrote that he sought "to discover the interaction between the forces of nature and the influence that environmental geography has on plant and animal life." But the nineteenth century was a turning point in the development of environmental awareness. In 1823, Jacques Arago observed with alarm the destruction of giant trees in the Pacific which had taken hundreds of years to grow; while in 1832, George Catlin, a lawyer and painter of aboriginal people, expressed great concern at the decline of buffalo vital to the survival of these people and demanded a government policy to establish national parks. In 1859, Isidore Geoffroy-Saint-Hilaire, a professor at the Museum of Natural History and at the Faculty of Science in Paris, defined a new discipline devoted to: "the study of the relationship of organised beings in the family and society, and in their wholeness (aggregate) and community". He called this discipline 'ethology'.[2] In the same year, the German biologist Ernest Haeckel used the term ecology to describe "the science of the relationships between organisms and the environment in the largest sense, taking all conditions into consideration." Again during the same year, Charles Darwin in England raised questions about the relationship between animals and plants, illustrating the problem with his renowned example of the drone bee and the clover patch. A decade later, Ernest Haeckel gave a lecture in Jena refining his first definition of ecology to encompass "the economy of nature" and "the research of all the relations between animals and their environment, inorganic and organic, which implies both amicable and hostile relations with animals and planets with which these are in direct or indirect contact."[3] In 1864, George Perkins Marsh published *Man and Nature or Physical Geography as modified by Human Action*, a pioneering study of the Mediterranean basin which included prescient observations of environmental deterioration. In 1877, the geographer and anarchist teacher Elisée Reclus warned of the degradation of the environment by human beings in his celebrated *Nouvelle Géographie universelle*. In 1885, Vladimir de Schoenefeld wrote eloquently in Fontainebleu about the despoliation of the environment affecting many species.

Origins Of Environmentalism

The term 'environmentalism' is used in this text to refer to an approach which, like acute medicine, deals with crises only as they arise. It tends to be biased towards the concerns of an elite group, proposing reforms which will make life more pleasant for the already privileged but neglecting the problem of social and economic inequality. It also tends to assume that the best we on this planet can do is to survive, ignoring the potential for a creative and fruitful symbiosis between human beings and nature. Within the environmentalist current are the preservationists, who essentially want to protect things as they are, a view which ignores the importance of dynamic balance or homeostasis. A part of this current grew into conservationism which promotes the carefully planned use of natural resources — both biotic and abiotic — and elements of our historical heritage, in order to ensure that no unnecessary harm is done to them. It seeks to ensure the continued survival of particular resources such as areas of land or species of wildlife.

The development of the discipline of natural history brought to light our civilization's exploitation of nature. Among one segment of society there arose a growing concern with the protection of wildlife, followed by demands for the preservation of sectors of rural areas to offset increasing urbanisation. In Britain, the growth of botany, zoology, and natural history generally, from the sixteenth century forward, created the foundations of environmentalism in that country. The work of people like Gilbert White, Thomas Bewick, Carl von Linne, John Ray, Darwin, and Wallace, all contributed, along with the poetry of Woodsworth, to an environmental awakening.

In Victorian times, the study of natural history was thought to bring one closer to God, as well as providing the tools to conquer nature with science and technology. Progress meant mastery over nature. The work of Darwin, however, offered support for the view that natural evolution placed human beings and other species in the same sphere, and that this kinship enjoined humans to protect the environment from abuse.

By the 1880's, there were hundreds of natural history associations in England with thousands of members. At about the same time in France, the French association for the Protection of Nature (SNPN) and the French Federation of Associations for the Protection of Nature (FFSPN) were founded.

The same morality which infused the antislavery movement also influenced British environmentalism. The year 1824 witnessed the establishment of the Society for the Prevention of Cruelty to Animals. The British parliament passed laws to protect sea birds (1869), wild birds (1872), and wild fowl (1876). On the continent, a convention took place in Berlin in 1885 on fishing salmon in the Rhineland and an international convention was held in Paris in 1895 with the goal of establishing protection for birds. Opposition to the killing of birds for the plumage used in fashionable clothing and hats was led by women in the mid 1880's and their protest led to the founding of a variety of organisations in Britain and the colonies. The feather boycott resulted in the passage of legislation against trade with India in such wildlife and ultimately in the banning of such exports from India by the colonial government.

In 1893, the National Trust was established to acquire country land to protect Britain's cultural and natural heritage from the spread of industrial towns. Capitalism was having a devastating impact on urban social conditions and many critics including Charles Dickens and Friedrich Engels were depicting its negative effects on human health, on moral and social values, and on the physical environment. The protection of certain urban commons and rural areas was intended to make such space available for public use, as well as to preserve plants and animals.

The science of forestry was most advanced in Germany at this time and it played an important role in the growth of conservationism worldwide. British colonialism in India was bent on the profitable exploitation of India's forests to enhance State revenues. As early as 1847, the British brought in German foresters to pursue this objective. But in Australia, also a British colony, no such scientific management was engaged and the clear cutting of forests went on in the most rapacious manner. During the 1660's in Africa — and especially in southern Africa — European colonialism resulted in the reckless clearance of forests, the rapacious killing of animals for skins and other treasures (for example, hippopotamae for their teeth, rhinocerae for their horns, elephants for their ivory, ostriches for their feathers). By the nineteenth century certain protective measures were enshrined in law, with limited effect. In the early 1870's, 2500 elephants were hunted down, yielding 50 tons of ivory, and in the single year of 1876 some 900 were killed. Some game reserves were established, like the Kruger National Park, but the effect was marginal. During the same period, soil erosion, drought and associated problems were observed. However, what warnings were issued were generally ignored unless profits were in peril.

In the USA by the 1700's roughly 200,000 hectares of woods were cleared for farming in

New England.[4] Sixty percent of the forests of Massachusetts were cleared by 1880. In the pattern of settlement of the country was reflected the instrumental attitude towards nature characteristic not only of capitalism but of the Judeo-Christian heritage.

The alarum was sounded by numerous scientists, from J.J. Audubon to John Muir, and by philosophers such as Ralph Waldo Emerson and Henry David Thoreau. But it was the publication in 1864 of George Perkins Marsh's book *Man and Nature* which precipitated the establishment of a national forestry commission. At the same time, the U.S. Congress set aside certain areas for recreational enjoyment as part of its land management plan; for example, Yosemite Valley and the Mariposa Grove were conditionally given to the State of California.

A decade later in 1872, 800,000 hectares were set aside to create the Yellowstone National Park, the world's first such preserve. In 1879 the Royal National Park was established in Australia, in 1885 the Banff National Park in Canada, and in 1894 the Tongariro National Park in New Zealand. The motives for these laudable measures were mixed, ranging from national prestige, to wilderness preservation, to creating areas for public recreation.

By the 1900's a controversy had arisen in the U.S. between the preservationists influenced by British protectionism and the conservationists influenced by German forestry. The former wanted wilderness areas to be set aside for recreational and educational purposes only, while the latter wished to exploit nature rationally — read profitably. The protagonists in this debate were John Muir, the naturalist who founded the Sierra Club in 1892 (and who was something of a religious zealot in his literal worship of nature), and Gifford Pinchot, a wealthy student of German forestry who favoured the planned commercial exploitation of woodlands. The conflict was confined to a narrow circle of professionals and self-appointed guardians of the public good, which they often conflated with their own particular interests.

A number of State management measures were introduced in the U.S. under the Democratic presidency of Theodore Roosevelt. In 1907 the Inland Waterways Commission was established at the prompting of Pinchot who recognised the importance of hydroelectric power, water transportation, and flood and erosion control. The same year saw the creation of the National Conservation Commission headed by Pinchot. It was short-lived because of Congressional fear of growing presidential powers. The Republicans were waiting in the wings, Taft was soon to become President. Under Roosevelt, however, Pinchot was able in 1909 to organise the first North American Conservation Congress, which he chaired and which drew together delegates from Canada, Newfoundland, Mexico and the U.S. This Congress concluded that it was essential to approach conservation from a transnational perspective. Another effort to organise a meeting of countries extending beyond North America was shelved by President Taft whose Republican administration did not manifest the same interest in environmentalism as the Democrats.

The United States was not the only nation in which efforts were made to promote conservation. Conservationists elsewhere also sought to establish certain rules. In 1900 a conference for the protection of African mammals was held in London; in 1902 a convention on the protection of birds took place in Paris. But these gatherings expressed concern with protection primarily in the aim of serving human interests. The narrow anthropocentric character of the protectionist approach was reflected in the first international agreement to protect animals which was signed in Vienna in 1868 and limited to the protection of those animals useful to agriculture and forestry. By 1902 this agreement had been signed by twelve European countries.

Furthermore, it was hunters and naturalists who sponsored the establishment in 1903 of the Society for the Preservation of the Wild Fauna of the Empire, dedicated to the protection of animal life in the British colonies (the first such international organisation). For one of the most interesting examples of the conflict between the aims of wildlife preservation and those of the protection of animals central to human use we must look to the period following the First World War. Almost half a million wild animals were killed in Southern Rhodesia alone in the post-war period because colonial authorities wanted to protect domestic stocks from disease as part of an anti-tsetse fly campaign.

Prior to the presidency of Franklin D. Roosevelt, conservationism had become associated with the capitalist interests around the Republican Party. But the Democratic Party in government was more sincerely committed to environmental protection. Using the power of the State to bring about economic recovery during the Great Depression, it created the Tennessee Valley Authority and the Civilian Conservation Corps, deploying the unemployed in flood control, forestry and soil erosion prevention efforts. Preservationism underwent a renewal under the Democratic administration. In 1934 almost seven million people visited national parks; four years later these parks attracted 17 million visitors. The federal State sought to create greater public access to the parks — which granted temporary psychological relief to the people of the overpopulated eastern States. Wilderness enthusiasts, however, objected to having more roads being built into the parks.

It was also during the Roosevelt years that the most massive environmental disaster to date occurred in the U.S. Hundreds of dust storms ripped across the Great Plains, some blocking all sunlight and leaving six meter high drifts driving dust from the Atlantic to Chicago. These storms were the result of over half a century of agriculture which ploughed long straight furrows and relied on a single crop, giving rise to the deterioration of sod — an important buffer to wind and drought — and leaving fields bare of vegetation. Some 1.3 million square kilometres of top soil had been eroded and the country was forced to import wheat. In its 1936 report, the Great Plains Committee concluded that the single-minded pursuit of profits, unregulated competition, and the notion that nature could be completely subjugated to human will, would lead to a serious environmental disequilibrium.[5]

In Europe around the same time, the establishment of national nature organisations in France and Belgium in 1925-1926 and the creation of the Netherlands Committee for International Nature Protection revived calls for the establishment of a large inter-State body to address environmental concerns. By 1934, *l'Office International pour la Protection de la Nature* was established, but the initiative was derailed by the advent of the Second World War.

During the war years, some international consultation took place with the aim of planning for the conservation of natural resources and the re-establishment of a transnational organisation. The American conservationists stepped up their pressure, so that by 1944 there was a recognition on the part of State agencies and the political parties that conservation would have to be an essential part of the new post-war world order. However, conflicting agendas impeded these efforts. For example, the basic aim of the Anglo-American Petroleum agreement was the development of world petroleum resources, whereas the new U.N. Economic and Social Council (ECOSOC) wanted energy conservation to be a key to postwar economic planning. The U.S. State Department and the individuals around the Anglo-American petroleum deal pursued an essentially self-serving agenda, while the scientific circles around the United Nations were attempting to reflect broader interests.

After The United Nations

In spite of numerous setbacks and ideologically charged conflicts, the post-war period saw some real victories for the conservation movement. By 1946, the Americans were urging ECOSOC to convene a scientific conference in the U.S. to "consider the conservation and effective utilization of natural resources." And in 1949, the United Nations Scientific Conference on the Conservation and Utilization of Resources (UNSCCUR) was held.

The Food and Agricultural Organisation (FAO) of the U.N. was founded in Québec in 1945. It focused on the development and exploitation of natural resources with a view to solving nutrition problems by improving the production and distribution of food. FAO's earliest efforts reflected the limits of a conservationist perspective insofar as they were driven as much by the goal of controlling and managing world agricultural production as by broader humanitarian aims.

In the background loomed the politics of hunger, population and land. The Great Depression had given a renewed lease on life to the dire prognostications of Malthus. In the immediate post war period, books like *The World's Hunger* by Pearson and Harper, *Our Plundered Planet* by Fairfield Osborn, and *Road to Survival* by William Voght were publishing, meditat on the implications of unchecked population growth in conditions of limited resources; they wondered how the Earth could possibly meet the needs of a growing population. Voght, an avowed neo-Malthusian, became a best-seller. He insisted that the U.S. was self-indulgent, over-populated, wasteful and doomed. His warnings were soon eclipsed as the U.S. economy burst into a boom of material production and consumption. However, Voght's assertion that the country was running low on resources did eventually lead to the founding in 1952 of "Resources for the Future", an organisation heavily influenced by trade and business organisations that had their own particular angle on conservation.

International Organisational Efforts To Protect Nature

The Europeans, especially the Swiss, Belgians and Dutch, worried that the newly founded U.N. was disproportionately influenced by Anglo-American interests. A tug of war ensued over how to manage the environment which lasted several decades. Europe was driven above all by a desire to progress through its postwar economic reconstruction and re-assert itself in the world economy.

From the International Office for the Protection of Nature (IOPN), to the founding in 1946 of the United National Educational, Scientific and Cultural Organisation (UNESCO), the international politics of environmentalism was marked by struggles over what kind of growth to encourage and over whose interests growth would favour. There were some generational conflicts as well, with the older European school tending towards a preservationist approach, while many new American scholars favoured more environmental research. There was also considerable vying for position, with various organisations each seeking to establish itself as the dominant environmental protection agency.

Among UNESCO's mandates was the promotion of international exchanges of scientific research. Interestingly, in 1947 UNESCO's Department of Natural Science began to research and circulate scientific data on the Amazon forest. At its general conference that same year, it took a small step forward when it expounded the idea that nature could not be divorced from culture and that the preservation of rare and interesting plants and animals was a vital part of scientific endeavour.

Also in 1947 IOPN facilitated the establishment of a Provisional International Union for the Protection of Nature (IUPN). Formally founded a year later, the IUPN sought to encourage cooperation in public education, regional planning, scientific research, preservation of wildlife and its habitats through the creation of protected areas, and scientific research bringing together governments, and concerned national and international organisations. Its constitution reveals an overlap between preservation and conservation perspectives. It was the dominant assumption of the organisation that nature existed to serve human ambitions and that conservation was meant to assist in the fulfillment of this goal.

Conservation efforts necessitated the gathering and compilation of the most complete information about the state of the environment on an ongoing basis. And it was to this end that the United Nations Scientific Conference on the Conservation and Utilization of Resources (UNSCCUR) was held in the U.S. in 1949. Jointly organised by U.N. agencies such as the World Health Organisation (WHO), the Food and Agricultural Organisation (FAO) and the International Labour Organisation (ILO), the conference brought together a total of 500 delegates from some 49 countries (excluding the Soviet Union). Marked by an atmosphere of optimism about the unlimited power of science to discover and create new resources, the main purpose of this gathering was to take stock of and exchange information about natural resources. Every imaginable question was dealt with: fuels and energy, water, minerals, forests, interdependence of resources, food, and all applied technologies. Engaging in what they deemed politically neutral scientific discussions, participants at the conference assiduously avoided overtly political issues, although in the tense climate of the Cold War there were obvious questions which might have been raised about the potential and actual political benefits of the scientific research being conducted. But, in fact, most States did not regard this kind of conference as politically valuable; it was only when many governments began to develop environmental protection programmes that such conferences took on greater political significance as with the Biosphere Conference in 1968 and the Stockholm Conference in 1972.

By the mid 50's scientists had come to dominate the IUPN. Dedicating itself, unlike UNESCO, primarily to the protection of nature, it changed its name in 1956, largely due to American pressure, to the International Union for Conservation of Nature and Natural Resources (IUCN), although the name change did nothing to alter the organisation's preservationist bias. In 1960 a twin body to IUCN was founded called the World Wildlife Fund (WWF) which was devoted to raising large sums of money for projects designed to protect wilderness and wildlife. A disproportionate amount of the money raised by this organisation was spent in North America and Europe; the other three continents received 15 per cent of the funds. Eventually, under criticism by donors for its Eurocentric approach, the IUCN began to sponsor projects to preserve areas of wild nature in Asia.

The colonializing States of the northern hemisphere also retained an interest in the African environment in the post-colonial period. Indeed, conservationists were eager to encourage the new African states to conserve natural vegetation, soil, water, and natural resources. For instance, when the Third International Conference for the Protection of the Fauna and Flora of Africa took place, in Bukavu, (in the Belgian Congo) in 1953, the IUCN initiated the African Special Project and a series of studies and conferences were organised. The new national governments were told that they had to plan for the rational exploitation of nature, and that such planning would be conducive to international aid. Furthermore, the IUCN provided specialists to advise interested African States and drafted the agreement which was adopted in 1967 by the Organisation of African Unity (OAU) as the African Convention for Conservation of Nature and Natural Resources, which came into effect in 1969.

From the post-war period to the 1960's, then, conservation was clearly the reigning ideology of environmentalists and was given expression in a multiplicity of programmes and projects.

The Road To Stockholm And Rio

By the late 1960's environmentalism had gained a good deal of momentum. Not only had the warnings of various writers had a decisive public impact, but accumulated scientific research and a series of environmental disasters pointed to a problem of increasingly alarming proportions.

In 1962, under the pen name Lewis Herber, Murray Bookchin published *Our Synthetic Environment* a comprehensive examination of the deleterious environmental effects of industrial development and technology, from air pollution to contaminated milk and the misuse of chemical pesticides. Six months later Rachel Carson published *The Silent Spring* — a simpler text by contrast, focusing on the single issue of pesticides, and especially DDT. Although there had been forecasts of the potentially dangerous environmental impact of these products as far back as 1945, they did not gain the same wide public attention as Carson's message. *Silent Spring* was serialized in the New Yorker magazine and became a best-seller, selling over half a million copies in its cloth-bound edition alone. By 1963, it was published in 15 countries. It also became the target of criticism in official political and corporate circles, as both State authorities and industry feared the public outcry the book aroused. But Carson's was only the first of a series of works on environmental degradation to gain a wide public hearing. Her basic message was echoed in the United States by Paul Ehrlich, Barry Commoner, Lamont Cole, Eugene Odum, Kenneth Watt, and Garret Hardin. The cumulative effect of the work of these pioneers on public consciousness was palpable; in April 1970 the largest demonstration in history calling for the protection of the environment took place when roughly 300,000 Americans turned out to mark Earth Day.

In 1972, *The Limits to Growth* was published. This report had its roots in the 1940s and the seminal studies of Jay Forrester, an academic at the Massachusetts Institute of Technology. Forrester devised a forecasting methodology which had applications in the areas of digital computers, tactical military decision-making and information-feedback systems, as well as studies of the interacting forces of social systems. But the 1972 report was an initiative of the Club of Rome, an organisation of technocrats, scientists, economists, politicians and industrialists from 25 countries. A precursor to the Trilateral Commission.[6] its objective was to study the emerging global system in all its aspects — political, environmental, social, and economical. Forrester's work at M.I.T. was used to develop the global modelling techniques employed in the writing of the report.

The Limits to Growth contributed to conservationism the idea that the environmental crisis is rooted in exponential economic growth. The report predicted that by the end of the century the cumulative effects of pollution, food shortages, and the exhaustion of natural resources, would spell disaster. Among the remedies it proposed were a 40 per cent reduction in the birth rate, a 40 per cent reduction in industrial investment, a 20 per cent reduction in agricultural investment and a substantial transfer of wealth from the rich countries to poor ones.

The Limits to Growth had its parallel in Britain in *Blueprint for Survival*, which was also based on the premise that the combined effects of continuing population growth and the depletion of natural resources demanded changes in human practices. However, while *Limits to Growth* was oriented toward government measures, *Blueprint* underscored the need for a reevaluation of received attitudes at the base of society.

By the late 1970s, some four million copies of *The Limits to Growth* had been sold in 30 languages. But the conclusions of the report did not go unchallenged. For instance, researchers at the Science Policy Research Unit of the University of Sussex in Britain issued a report which drew attention to the weaknesses of the M.I.T. methodology and to the ideological values underpinning the analysis. The crucial problem, they concluded, was to assure more equal distribution of wealth and resources, but rather than simplistically calling for an end to growth, they placed emphasis on the quality of development. And their report underscored the importance of future technical progress, including, the development of nuclear power, without cautioning against this environmentally harmful technology.

The Limits to Growth was one of several studies to have a bearing on the U.N. Conference on the Human Environment held in Stockholm in 1972. In preparation for that conference, a research group at M.I.T. produced a Study of Critical Environmental Problems (SCEP), which discussed the effect on global climatic and terrestrial conditions of specific atmospheric, terrestrial, and marine pollutants and examined research and monitoring methods. This study declared that, "Currently, and in the foreseeable future, the advanced industrial societies will have to carry the load of remedial action against pollution." It went on to call for a more complete enquiry into marine oil pollution, atmospheric carbon dioxide build-up, and the negative effects of supersonic transportation.

The urgent tone of academic studies was both spurred and borne out by a series of environmental disasters which occurred between 1966 and 1972. Environmental crises were not, of course, unprecedented: in 1948, 20 people died and some 40 per cent of the population of Donora, Pennsylvannia became ill with the effects of sulphurous fog; in 1952 a winter fog in London resulted in the immediate deaths of 445 people, while an additional 4000 people died mostly from long-term circulatory or respiratory disorders. (It took another four years before the Clean Air Act was passed by the British House of Commons); in 1957, a fire erupted and burned for 85 hours at the Windscale nuclear power plant in northern England due to overheating. But beginning in the 1960's, the combination of mass media coverage and growing environmental consciousness intensified public awareness and concern.

In 1966 a pit-heap collapsed in Aberfan, South Wales, which left 144 dead (116 of them children) bearing witness to the hazards of abandoned land and pollution. In 1967, the tanker 'Torrey Canyon' spilled an estimated 875,000 barrels of crude oil off the southwest coastal tip of England. (In 1950 there was one oil tanker larger than 50,000 dead weight tons; a decade later there were over 600 tankers heavier than that.) The use of detergents to break down the oil caused further biological deterioration of the environment. The event shook public opinion to the extent that two years later a Royal Commission on Environmental Pollution was struck and two agreements were signed: the Convention Relating to Intervention on the High Seas in Cases of Oil Pollution Casualties and the Convention on Civil Liability for Oil Pollution Damage. In 1969 an oil blow out on a Union Oil Company platform off the coast of Santa Barbara, California caused great damage. It took two days to bring the blowout under initial control only to have it erupt again a few weeks later. The crisis lasted for weeks, and months later beaches were still polluted. The U.S. Secretary of the Interior ordered the immediate closing of all oil wells, but within 24 hours he allowed resumption of drilling and production.

In spite of laws and conventions, an estimated 10,000 annual spills of oil and other hazardous materials polluted the navigational waters of the U.S. alone during the late 1960's.[7] And by now all sorts of environmental catastrophes had begun to receive attention and come into public view: mercury pollution through chemical production in Minamata, Japan, leading to 857 deaths between 1953 and 1961; a gas explosion in Feyzin, France, in 1966 which left 45 dead; in 1976 in England at Windscale again 35 people died; in the same year in Seveso, Italy, 700 persons were evacuated due to dioxin poisoning; in 1978 in San Carlos, Spain, 200 people died due to an accident involving the transportation of gases; in 1979 200,000 people were evacuated at Three Mile Island in the U.S. as a result of nuclear reactor trouble; in the same year in Mississauga, Canada, a chlorine explosion after a train derailment required the evacuation of 220,000 people; in the same year, in Novossibirsk,

U.S.S.R., emissions of chemicals left 300 dead; in 1979 an accident on an oil-drilling platform in the Gulf of Mexico caused oil spilling for nine months; in 1982, in Caracas, Venezuela, a petroleum explosion resulted in 101 deaths; in 1983, in Tacoa, an explosion of stored gas left 153 dead, and the casualty list continues ...

Although there was no dearth of international meetings and conferences during this period, the Intergovernmental Conference of Experts on the Scientific Basis for Rational Use and Conservation of the Resources of the Biosphere held in 1968 under the sponsorship of UNESCO was of particular significance. Paving the way for Stockholm, more than a third of the recommendations of this conference called for more environmental research and education.

But the culminating point of the growing recognition of the importance of State management of the growing environmental crisis was the United Nations Conference on the Human Environment, held in Stockholm in 1972. This conference also revealed a perceived need to absorb or coopt the energy of various lobbies demanding more environmental regulation before supporters of these campaigns became too political. The Stockholm conference led to the establishment of the United Nations Environmental Programme (UNEP), which reflected the collective perspectives of the governments of the more powerful developed nations and sought to incorporate the less developed countries and their politicians and bureaucrats into global conservation plans.

Whereas the 1968 conference focused on the collection of scientific data documenting the environmental crisis, the 1972 Stockholm conference shifted the inter-State agenda to the related political, economic and social problems. The conceptual framework of the conference was laid out in a report entitled *Only One Earth* produced a year earlier by Baroness Jackson of Lodsworth, the former assistant editor of *The Economist*, Barbara Ward, and an American biologist, René Dubos. This report was reviewed by 152 consultants from industry, science, and the academy. A rather dry and uninspired document, *Only One Earth* observed that pollution, the waste and misuse of land, the consumer society, urban sprawl, and the exhaustion of natural resources were 'problems of high technology' of the developed countries, whereas the problems of population, industry and pollution, chemicalized agriculture and urban growth were issues facing the less developed countries. The report was actually published by the International Institute for Environmental Affairs (IIEA) established by the Aspen Institute of Humanistic Studies in Colorado and chaired by Robert O. Anderson, head of the Atlantic Richfield oil company. After Stockholm the IIEA moved to London where it was headed by Barbara Ward.

The Stockholm conference gathered together representatives of 113 nation-States, 19 intergovernmental agencies, and 400 other intergovernmental and non-governmental organisations. With the exception of Roumania, the Soviet bloc was absent, supposedly because there was no agreement on the voting status of the German Democratic Republic. China, however, was present.

Political representatives from developing nations insisted that environmental protection must be balanced with economic development and growth. They looked askance at any measures which might impede the development of industrial capitalism and its attendant benefits at home. Both State environmental managers and the lobbyists from the NGOs had to agree that conservationism had to take an equitable form.

The U.S. government was an enthusiastic participant in the Stockholm conference. It sponsored a ten-year moratorium on commercial whaling, but opposed many positions advanced or supported by Third World delegations. The American delegation sought to weaken the proposed International Register of Potentially Toxic Chemicals, abstained from voting against nuclear weapons testing, and generally sought to dilute the substance of any U.N. environmental programme. Outside the meeting rooms the U.S. government was condemned for its war in Indochina and the human and environmental costs of that war.

The U.N. organisers sought to confine the environmentalist NGOs to an official Environmental Forum, designed, as many activists noted, to divert their attention away from the official proceedings and thus contain controversial questions. Anticipating such a manoeuver, the Swedish-based Pow Wow group organised a Folkets Forum

(People's Forum) in 1971. It expressed concern at the apparent neglect by the official conference of such critical issues as chemical and biological weapons production and the ecocide resulting from the U.S. war in Indochina. The underlying assumption of the participants in the People's Forum was that the official conference was en-meshed in irreconcilable contradictions because State representatives were beholden to vested in-terests in industry and government who stood to suffer from any far-reaching measures to stem the environmental crisis.[8] Not surprisingly, the NGOs had a very limited influence on the Stockholm conference, and in subsequent years many of these organisations concentrated on the work of public education and consolidating and extending their respective bases of support. In 1974, only about 150 NGOs attended the meeting of the Governing Council of UNEP (Stockholm's follow-up struc-ture) and by 1980 there were only 20 represented. By 1982 the U.N. Environmental Liaison Centre listed some 2,230 environmental NGOs in less developed countries, a 60 per cent increase since Stockholm, and some 13,000 in developed countries, a 30 per cent increase since that meeting. After 1972 too there was greater contact between NGOs across the world and more concerted action, giving form to a new political internationalism. These bonds were strengthened with increasing evidence of the ineffectuality of governmental ac-tion despite the pious rhetoric of 1972.

As the ruling interests became aware of the costs of the far-reaching changes necessary to protect the environment they attempted to divert attention away from the environmental crisis by focusing attention on the 1973-1974 energy crisis, declining economic rates of growth, and the unstable international situation symbolized by the Cold War. But as concerned citizens sought a deeper understanding of the environmental crisis they had developed a more holistic approach to understanding environmental problems. There was a growing awareness that environmental problems were related to specific forms of economic and social organisation, including the political structure of the State. The limited and limiting perspectives of preservationism and conservationism began to be transcended; the epoch of ecology was beginning; and the environmentalists who were not careerists and opportunists were rapidly learning from each other and creating more organisational links and networks.

In sum, the Stockholm conference had produced little more than a Declaration, a list of Principles and an Action Plan which represented an initial accommodation between the interests of the developed and less developed nation-States. The Stockholm conference was to be followed by a conference on population in 1974, on desertification in 1977, and on new and renewable energy sources in 1981. But Stockholm did result in one notable political achievement: the establishment of the United Nations Environment Programme (UNEP) 1972-1982, located in Nairobi, Kenya.

This body was composed of an international council for environmental programs, a secretariat to promote coordination within the U.N. system, and an environmental fund to which nation-States would voluntarily contribute monies.

UNEP created Earthwatch with a mandate for environmental management, that is, comprehensive planning in support of nature protection to preserve biological diversity. UNEP also helped to negotiate international agreements, such as the Bonn Convention on migratory species, the Convention on International Trade in Endangered Species of Wild Fauna and Flora, the Convention for the Protection of the Mediterranean Sea against Pollution (1976), the moratorium on whaling, among others and so on. Further, it set up an early warning system for environmental hazards and a system for reporting on the status of certain natural resources. Thus a process of regular reporting on environmental research, monitoring and assessment was initiated. The UNEP mandate also included education, public information and the training of environmental managers.

UNEP initiated the Mediterranean Action Plan, adopted by 16 nations located around the sea, which was designed to manage problems of pollution and coastal degradation. Similar regional action plans included the Red Sea (1976), the Kuwait area (1978), the West and Central African coast (1981) and the Southwestern Pacific (1982).

UNEP failed in its campaign against desertification (the degradation of land through human misuse resulting in the loss of fertility). Desertification is in part the legacy of colonialism, which forced subject nations to increase exports to meet the needs of the metropolitan more cheaply and to pay taxes, thus pushing peasants into cash crop farming. This pressure to export continued when the new nation-States became part of the international capitalist economy as debtors so that indigenous agricultural practices were further undermined, reducing soil fertility, increasing soil erosion and engendering mass human impoverishment. One-third of the earth's land mass is semidesert but still supports more than 600 million people; half of this land supporting 80 million people is thought by scientists to be in the process of complete desertification. Solutions to desertification were known in the 70's, but they represented a threat to various powerful interests and hence the economic and political obstacles were insurmountable for UNEP. Its projects failed with the result, for instance, that deforestation, overgrazing, and poorly designed and managed irrigation led to the drought in the Sahel 1968-1973 and later the famine of 1984-1986.

From the spring of 1984, when the media reports started appearing about Ethiopia, public fund-raising efforts began to multiply. By 1986 more than $100 million was raised by pop and rock musicians with the Band-Aid and Live-Aid concerts, and another $51 million by U.S.A. for Africa. Meanwhile the 1984-1986 famine spread to 20 countries and an estimated one million people died, 10 million abandoned their homes and lands looking for water, food, and fertile land. The

Western media, the main transmitter of information about the famine, hardly acknowledged that environmental degradation was the root cause of the crisis, much less that this resulted from ecologically unsound development plans largely imposed on the South by the ruling interests in the North. But even the extremely circumspect World Bank quietly admitted in 1984 that Africa's development policies had to change.

In October 1984, the U.N. initiated World Commission on Environment and Development held its inaugural meeting chaired by the social democratic prime minister of Norway Gro Harlem Brundtland. In 1987, the Commission published the report *Our Common Future*, which examined trends in, among other things, energy, food, industry, international economic relations and human settlements, and offered forecasts for the beginning of the new millenium.

The Brundtland report augered in the era of sustainable development. There was little actually new in the concept of sustainable development; foresters in Germany and India in the previous century and Pinchot, among others, at the beginning of our own century advocated the need to manage natural resources rationally. What the now trendy term sustainable development implied was that many opinion-making environmentalists approved of economic growth on the condition that environmental considerations were integrated into economic development plans.

Again and again the report called for better management. It also gave added impetus to the charge long advanced by the peace movement that the ongoing international arms race was a wasteful drain on human, financial and material resources which could otherwise be devoted to development and environmental protection.

Predictably, the recommendations of the Brundtland report were largely ignored, as their implementation would conceivably imperil the international economic system of industrial capitalism and its concomitant political structures.[9]

Twenty years after Stockholm to the month, 178 nation-States and 117 heads of States — 35,000 people in all, including 9000 journalists — attended the United Nations Conference on Environment and Development, otherwise known as the Earth Summit, in Rio de Janiero, Brazil. It is worth noting that this supposedly auspicious conference took place in the same city where, as Amnesty International reported, street children were being shot to death by vigilante groups — often composed of off-duty police officers — paid by local businessmen to clear the streets of 'nuisances'.

The Earth Summit unfolded in a carnival-like atmosphere, and it was ultimately decried by many observers as a non-event, a missed opportunity. Few were naive enough to have believed that the conference would accomplish anything of substance, even with respect to the minimal goal of managing the environmental crisis. And the scepticism has been given ample justification in the year that has elapsed since the conference.

Once again parallel to the official summit — and in the long-run of greater significance — were the meetings of thousands of environmentalists and ecologists from NGOs from around the world. Together they worked on a remarkable collection of alternative international treatises and established transnational networks for future work. This time the entire spectrum of this new social movement was present, from the New Agers to representatives of the Green political parties.[10]

The Earth Summit gave rise, of course, to the adoption of 'The Rio Declaration,' which enshrined the objective of sustainable development. But its 27 principles, a kind of green human rights charter, are couched in vague terms and difficult to translate into action. They are so broad and abstract as to constitute little more than a pious wish.

Then the Convention on Biodiversity was adopted. It seeks to protect endangered flora and fauna and declares that each nation-State will undertake its realisation. No timetable is indicated. The document accords the countries of the northern hemisphere a free hand in the biologically diverse regions of the southern hemisphere in exchange for royalties paid for all commercial exploitation and access to new biotechnologies and all products resulting from such research. The majority of countries signed this convention, the U.S. being a notable exception.

A Convention on Climate ought to been given top priority. Before Rio, the European Community had proposed an 'ecotax' on energy and on CO_2 emissions as a step towards combatting global warming. One of the preconditions was that the Americans and Japanese also accept this policy. The U.S. refused, however, and hence the proposal was shelved. So the most ambitious plan for the Earth Summit dissolved into an unenforceable moral commitment to stabilize CO_2 emissions by the year 2000.

A proposed Convention on Forests was reduced to a mere declaration because, in the name of national sovereignty, several exporters of tropical wood (Brazil, India, Malaysia, Indonesia) refused to be bound by it. Both producers and consumers are now simply requested to respect the heritage of the world's forests. As long as sustainable management is followed the logging of endangered species of trees can continue.

Agenda 21, a programme of more than 800 pages, invited the rich countries to help the poor ones along the path of sustainable development. To allow for a series of priority actions (drinkable water, reforestation, reversing soil erosion, among others), the more developed countries ought to increase international development aid to 0.7% of their Gross National Product (GNP) — a step they have been promising to take since 1970. Only the Scandinavian countries and the Netherlands accomplished this objective and now want to surpass it. France and Belgium promised to attain this goal by the year 2000, while the U.S. and Japan prefer to continue with what they call bi-lateral aid.

Thus the Rio Earth Summit also passed into history. In 1886 the first international agrement on the environment was signed. Today there are more than 250 such agreements, three-quarters of them signed since 1960. The first State pollution agency was created some 125 years ago. In the 20 years preceding the publication of the Brundtland report more than 130 nation-States established environmental agencies and more than 180 international agreements had been signed. (A 1984 UNEP register documents 108 international agreements (see Table 1) and a 1985 update lists 257 multilateral treaties.[11]) Thousands of NGOs had been formed; 113 national delegations were sent to Stockholm; and the United Nations had its own international environmental programme. How have all these efforts to promote State management of the environment improved the ecological health of the Earth? The survey of the current state of the global environment in the following chapter would suggest that the impact of these initiatives has been far too limited.

As the bureaucrats, politicians, and environment managers were shaking hands good-bye, the departing ecologists at the alternative summit were reminding themselves of the ongoing tragedy in the Amazon, not far from Rio. We know how important tropical forests are to the Earth's ecology and that there is widespread public concern about these forests. Sixty per cent are found in South Africa and 33 per cent in Brazil. Recall who is behind Amazonian deforestation: twenty U.S. multinational corporations, among them Union Carbide, Massey Ferguson,

Table 1.
International Conventions, Protocols, Treaties and Amendments Relating to the Environment: 1911-1983

Subject	Year Signed							
	1911-20	21-30	31-40	41-50	51-60	61-70	71-80	81-83
Pollution including marine	—	—	—	—	1	5	19	6
Marine/fisheries	—	—	—	3	8	4	10	5
Nature & natural resources	1	—	2	1	—	1	3	—
Toxic substances including radiation	—	1	—	—	3	4	2	—
Animals	—	—	—	1	1	1	6	—
Regional development	—	—	—	—	1	2	4	—
Insects pests	—	—	—	—	—	4	—	—
Plants	—	—	—	—	4	—	—	—
Ecosystems	—	—	—	—	—	—	2	—
Birds	—	—	—	—	1	1	—	—
Environments	—	—	—	—	—	—	1	—
Total	1	1	2	5	19	22	47	11

Source: United Nations Environment Programe, *Resgister of International Treaties and Other Agreements in the Field of the Environment.* (UNEP/ GC/ INFO/11) Nairobi: UNEP, May 1984.

Chrysler, Ford and Bethlem Steel; ten Japanese multinationals including Mitsubishi, Toshiba, Sony, Suzuki; six German multinationals, for example, Volkswagen and Bosch; five Italian multinationals, Ferrari, Fiat, Pirelli ...; three British multinationals; and the Swiss group Nestlé. And the mineral riches from the Grande Carajas project have already been divided up, three hundred years in advance, between Japanese, U.S. and West European multinationals. But these silent partners of the State representatives at Rio were not officially present at the Earth Summit.

Notes

1. See *Fields, Factories and Workshops*, first published in 1899. Republished by (Montréal/New York: Black Rose Books, 1994) Introduction by George Woodcock.

2.. *Histoire naturelle dés régnes organiques*, Volume II, (Paris: Masson, 1859).

3. "Ueber Entwickelungsgang und Aufgabe der Ecologie" Jenaische Zeits, (F. Naturwissenschaft, 1870).

4. Worster, Donald, *Nature's Economy*, (San Francisco: Sierra Club Books, 1977), p. 67.

5. Great Plains Committee, *"The Future of the Great Plains"*, (Washington, D.C., U.S. Government Printing Office, 1936).

6. See *Trilateralism*, The Trilateral Commission and Elite Planing for World Management, edited by Holly Sklar, Montréal/New York: Black Rose Books, 1980).

7. Council on Environmental Quality, *"Environmental Quality 1970"* (Washington, D.C., U.S. Government Printing Office, 1970), p. 38.

8. Haley, Jean Mary, ed., *"Open Options: A Guide to Stockholm's Alternative Environmental Conferences,"* (Stockholm, 1972).

9. Clow, Micheal, *Ecological Exhaustion and the Global Crisis* of *Capitalism,* (Montréal: Our Generation, Volume 23, Number 1, 1992).

10. See *Les Traités Alternatif de Rio*, (Montréal: Editions Ecosociété, 1994).

11. Burhenne, Wolfgang, ed., *International Environmental Law: Multilateral Treaties*. (Berlin: E. Schmidt Verlag, 1985).

The Ecological Crisis and
the Response of Citizens to
the Plight of the Earth

Section Two

The Ecological Crisis
and the Response of Citizens
to the Plight of the Earth

The most dangerous threat to our global environment may not be the strategic threats themselves but rather our perception of them, for the most people do not yet accept the fact that this crisis is extremely grave.

U.S. Vice-President Al Gore, 1992

By the end of the last decade, few speeches made by the heads of States of the developed nations would fail to invoke the environmental crisis, and corporate executives began to declare themselves committed environmentalists. But it is one thing to establish international treatises, national laws, and environment ministries and agencies; it is quite another to effect the concrete changes in attitudes, practices and institutions necessary to resolve the ecological crisis. It is true that, to date, there have been environmental improvements, at least temporarily, in a few critical areas. But overall the scientific indicators paint a grim picture.

Despite the substantial growth of environmental awareness among people throughout the world, the health of the Earth continues to deteriorate at an unprecedented rate. Here we can only sketch the contours of the problem; more ample documentation is readily available in hundreds of reports and books published in many countries and in most languages.

Since 1972, the year of the Stockholm conference, deserts have expanded by 120 million hectares, claiming more land than that under cultivation in Nigeria and China combined. The area is as large as the United States east of the Mississippi River. Thousands of plants and animal species have ceased to exist since 1972. Over 500 billion tons of topsoil have been lost to the farmers of the planet, an area almost the size of the agricultural land of India and France combined. According to the National Coalition Against the Misuse of Pesticides, the U.S. is producing pesticides today at a rate thirteen thousand times faster than when *Silent Spring* was published.

By the end of the 1980's, the world's forests were being reduced by an estimated 17 million hectares each year, up from 11 million hectares at the beginning of that decade. As the demand for lumber, paper, and firewood soared, and as the need for cropland increased, the pace of deforestation has been stepped up. Some countries, such as Ethiopia and Mauritania, have lost nearly all their woods. Thailand and the Ivory Coast will have little left by the end of the 1990's.

Every year, some six million hectares of land are so severely damaged that they are lost to production, becoming wasteland. Topsoil is lost to wind and water erosion, deforestation and over-grazing. Hundreds of cities are afflicted with persistent air pollution, and this problem is now affecting rural areas. Breathing air in some cities like Bombay is equivalent to smoking 10 cigarettes a day, and in Mexico City it is considered life-threatening. Two million cars and the use of low-grade leaded gasoline in Bangkok have added 38 different chemicals to the city's air. In 1990, over 1 million people were treated for respiratory problems; lead poisoning has reached epidemic proportions among the city's children, while the incidence of lung cancer is three times higher in the city than in the rest of the country. In other parts of the planet, air pollution and acid rain damage crops and forests. Many of Europe's forests are already dead, others continue to deteriorate. In the northeastern part of North America, the sugar maple of Canada and the U.S. have been experiencing stunted growth for some years, and foresters have concluded that it is too late to reverse the process. As China now surpasses the U.S. as the world's leading coal burner, the damage to Chinese forests is massive. In his book *Earth in the Balance,* U.S. Vice-President Al Gore writes:

Some of the successes in dealing with air quality have created new problems. For example, the use of tall smokestacks to reduce local air pollution has helped to worsen regional problems like acid rain. The higher the air pollution, the farther it travels from its source. Some of what used to be Pittsburgh's smoke is now Labrador's acidic snow. Some of what Londoners used to curse as smog now burns the leaves of Scandinavian trees.

And while many of the measures that control local and regional air pollution also help reduce the global threat, many others actually increase that threat. For example, energy-consuming 'scrubbers' used to control acid precipitation, now cause the release of even more carbon dioxide (CO_2) into the atmosphere. A power plant fitted with scrubbers will produce approximately 6 percent more global air pollution in the form of CO_2 for each BTU of energy generated. Moreover, the sulphur emissions from coal plants partly offset, and temporarily conceal, the regional effects of the global warming these plants help to produce worldwide.[1]

The U.S. Environmental Protection Agency (EPA) reported in 1988 that ground water in 39 States contained pesticides. In 1990, the agency reported some 100,000 violations of its water quality standards. The EPA now claims that almost half of all rivers, lakes and creeks are still damaged or threatened by water pollution. At least half the river water in Poland is too polluted for industrial use. South Korea's Naktong River has become a helpless victim of that country's massive industrialization: in 1990 alone, some 343 factories illegally dumped toxic wastes into the waters. Thousands of people became violently ill in the city of Taegu when they consumed drinking water containing phenol, a chemical used in processing circuit boards for computers. The ocean explorer Jacques Cousteau claims that pollution in the oceans has now damaged the very thin membrane on the ocean's surface — neuston — which helps capture and stabilize the food supply for the tiniest sea organisms, phytoplankton, which forms the neuston and which begins the food chain.

The effects of water pollution are the worst in the developing countries. More then 1.7 billion people do not have access to safe drinking water, causing death from cholera, typhoid, dysentery, and diarrhoea from both viral and bacteriological sources. More than three billion people do not have proper sanitation systems and thus incur the risk of contaminated water. The huge Aral Sea basin in the former Soviet Union is virtually dead. The accumulation of agricultural pesticides in local water supplies causes birth defects, miscarriages, kidney damage, and cancer. The incidence of oesophageal cancer is seven times the national level. But this is only a fraction of the picture: a 1987 estimate calculated the country's health costs at 190 billion rubles, or 11 per cent of the gross national product at that time.

In 1991, atmospheric measurements made by the U.S. National Aeronautics and Space Adminstration indicated that the Earth's protective ozone layer is being depleted at twice the rate scientists had calculated, and by four to five per cent over the U.S. in a 13-year period. Research by scientists has recently concluded that 200,000 additional deaths from skin cancer could occur in the U.S. alone during the next 50 years. In *Earth in the Balance*, U.S. Vice-President Al Gore writes:

> Of course, the history of climate change is also the history of human adaptation to climate change. During the subsistence crisis of 1816-1817, for example, the bureaucratic, administrative tendencies of the modern State were given great impetus. In virtually every European country, central governments organized and distributed the scarce supplies of food and imported new stocks from Odessa, Constantinople, Alexandria, and America. For the first time, large-scale public work projects were organized chiefly to provide employment in the hope of staving off the popular disturbances and food riots that accompanied the subsistence crisis. In the 1930s, the Dust Bowl was among the many disruptive social and economic problems that led to an even more complex version of the administrative state, Franklin Roosevelt's New Deal.

> All of these changes in climate patterns took place during temperature variations of only 1 to 2 degrees Centigrade. Yet today, at the close of the twentieth century, we are in the process of altering global temperatures by up to three to four times that amount and causing changes in climate patterns that are likely to have enormous impacts on global civilization. Among the most dramatic effects, if the historical record is any guide, will be massive

migrations of people from areas where civilization is disrupted to other areas where they hope to find the means for survival and a better way of life — but with unpredictable consequences for those areas.[2]

The statistics which informed an international agreement to remove ozone-destroying chlorofluocarbons (CFCs) by the year 2000 are now thought to be too conservative. If CFC production stopped immediately, ozone depletion would continue for another 20 to 30 years. It would take decades for the upper atmosphere to recover. CFCs have been produced for fewer than 60 years and yet they have already had a dramatic effect on the atmosphere. What about the effect of mass production of the other 20,000 chemical compounds introduced every year? Few are extensively tested for environmental effects before being used, although, ironically, CFCs were.

During the last decade, the amount of carbon pushed into the atmosphere from the burning of fossil fuels had reached six billion tons. The increasing concentration of this and other greenhouse gases, largely produced by industrial countries, is projected by scientists to rapidly increase global average temperature in coming decades. It is too early to establish the greenhouse effect conclusively, but the last decade was the warmest one registered since record keeping began more than a century ago.

At the local, regional and global levels the devastation of the biological diversity of the planet continues unabated. Biologists find it difficult to calculate accurately the number of plant and animal species that were lost during the last decade. But they do predict that one fifth of the species on Earth may disappear in the next two decades. What cannot be calculated at this time is how long such a rate of extinction can persist before ecosystems begin to collapse.

Since the Stockholm conference, the world population has increased by 1.6 billion. Another 90 million people are born every year. During the same period the world economy has grown by nearly 75 per cent, placing historically unparalleled demands on the Earth's limited resources.

The revolution in chemical production and use continues with awesome speed. In 1930, one million tons of chemicals were produced; in 1950, seven million tons; in 1970, 63 million tons; in 1990, 500 million tons. World production is doubling every seven to eight years. In the U.S. alone there are an estimated 650,000 commercial and industrial sources of hazardous waste. According to UNEP, more than seven million chemicals have now been discovered or created,and every year several thousand new ones are added. Of the 80,000 now in common use in large quantities, most produce chemical waste and most are hazardous. Many new chemical waste compounds are never tested for potential toxicity. The amount of this waste dumped into landfills, lakes, rivers, and oceans is staggering.

Industrial capitalism, in both its free-market and State capitalist guises, has created a civilization of the mass production of garbage. In the

U.S. alone, every person produced more than twice his or her weight in garbage every single day. The industrial countries are the greatest producers of garbage, but the mountains of garbage are also on the rise all over the world. Waste managers offer two basic solutions: landfills and incineration. Landfills are a limited option. Of the 20,000 landfills in existence in the U.S. in 1979, more than 15,000 have since been closed, having been filled to permanent capacity. So waste managers are now busy promoting incineration. Again in the U.S., almost always the trendsetter, municipal waste incinerated from 7 per cent in 1985 to over 15 per cent in 1989, and is expected to double again in the next several years.

A huge investment (almost $20 billion) in new incinerators is underway, as companies producing nuclear reactors are switching products. According to the U.S. congressional investigators, the air pollution from incinerators typically includes dioxins, furans, and pollutants like arsenic, cadmium, chlorobenzenes, chlorophenols, chromium, cobalt, lead, mercury, PCBs, and sulphur dioxide. In a lengthy study about mercury emissions the U.S. Clear Water Fund found that:

> Municipal waste incinerators are now the most rapidly growing source of mercury emissions to the atmosphere. Mercury emissions from incinerators [have] surpassed the industrial sector as a major source of atmospheric mercury are likely to double over the next five years. If the incinerators under con-

struction and planning come on line, with currently required control technology, mercury emissions from this source are likely to double. The growth will add millions of pounds of mercury to the ecosystem in the next few decades unless action is taken now.[3]

Toxic air pollution is only one part of the problem with garbage incineration. The new solid waste produced in the incineration process is in some ways an even more serious one. The some 10 per cent that remains as ash is highly toxic. Most municipalities do not treat this toxic ash as hazardous waste.

In 1992, the Royal Society of London and the U.S. National Academy of Science for the first time issued a joint report which began by stating:

If current predictions of population growth prove accurate and patterns of human activity on the planet remain unchanged, science and technology may not be able to prevent either irreversible degradation of the environment or continued poverty for much of the world.[4]

Although it was issued months before the Earth Summit, this extraordinary statement, which acknowledges that science and technology cannot ensure a better future unless population growth slows quickly and the world economy is restructured, had next to no impact on the proceedings at Rio. Technological optimism had underpinned the twentieth century's response to environmental problems. But now two of the world's important scientific organisations openly admit that we cannot rely on a "tech-no-fix." Clearly, the attempts at State manage-ment of the ecological crisis have yielded results which are questionable at best and we must con-clude that for a genuine reversal of global pat-terns to occur, more far-reaching political and economic changes in the dominant institutions of our society must be made. These fundamental changes must, moreover, be undertaken by our generation, as it may be too late for the next. Whether this generation will indeed be willing and able to take the necessary action 'from below' that our ruling elites have demonstrated themsel-ves reluctant to take remains an open and urgent question. But especially in the last 30 years or so, many citizens of nations West, East, North and South have become acutely aware of the immedi-ate and long-term consequences of environmen-tal deterioration and have begun to organise in one fashion or another in response to the plight of the Earth. And it is precisely to the variety of forms of popular response to the environmental crisis that we may now turn our attention.

It was estimated that in 1983 the British en-vironmental movement comprised some three million members (almost six per cent of the total population), making it the largest movement in that country's history.[5]

Table 2 lists the mainstream environmental organisations in Britain and the U.S. The table is, however, incomplete, failing to include thousands of national, regional and local or-ganisations, some falling within the mainstream

Table 2.

Membership of Selected British and U.S. Environmental Groups 1968-1984 (in thousands)

	1968	1972	1976	1980	1984
BRITIAN					
Royal Society for the Protection of Birds	41	108	204	300	340
Ramblers Association	15	26	30	32	37
National Trust	170	346	548	1000	1460*
Council for the Prodection of Rural England	16	25	28	29	30
Royal Society for Nature Conservation	35	75	109	140	180
TOTAL	277	580	919	1501	2047
UNITED STATES					
National Wildlife Federation	364	524	620	818	820
Sierra Club	68	136	165	182	348
Wilderness Society	39	67	91	50	65
National Audubon Society	66	164	269	400	450
Izaak Walton League	56	56	50	52	50
TOTAL	593	947	1195	1502	1733

Source: This figure is based on information from Francis Sandbach, *Environment: Ideology and Policy* (Oxford: Basil Blackwell, 1980), 12; *The Conservation Directory* (Washington, D.C.: National Wildlife Federation, various years).

*(*1982).*

of the movement and others of a more radical character. Still, it provides some indication of the scope of the movement in the Anglo-American part of the world.

It is important to realize, moreover, that environmental activism is not a phenomenon exclusive to the advanced industrial nations. We noted earlier that there are now more than 25,000 environmental organisations worldwide, according to some U.N. estimates. Alan B. Durning has

estimated that there are 100,000 such organisations, with 100,000 million members in the
developing nations alone.[6] According to the same
author,

> [In the Third World] people understand global
> degradation in its rawest forms. To them,
> creeping destruction of the ecosystem has
> meant lengthening workdays, failing
> livelihoods, and deteriorating health. And it
> has pushed them to act.[7]

The genesis of this new international social
movement is of particular interest to those concerned and committed to its objectives. From
about the mid-1960's into the 1970's a new generation of organisations emerged which created a tide
that dragged along the older established organisations. The moralistic preservationists and the
utilitarian conservationists now had to share the
stage with the new activists who became skilled
lobbyists and public opinion leaders. This new
social movement was far from homogeneous, em-
bodying a variety of ideological tendencies.

Like other social movements of the period,
the new activism was a response to powerful
historical forces developing before the 1960's.
Substantial changes took place in industrial
societies after the Second World War which
ushered in a period of intense economic growth
resulting in more widespread material affluence
and reinforcing a naive belief in perpetual and
penalty-free economic expansion. A near-
pathological consumerism fed a reckless
hedonism, so that the U.S., for instance, with six

per cent of the world's population, was producing and consuming over one-third of the world's goods and services by 1979. And yet there was discontent, especially among youth. For in the midst of this affluence many ugly contradictions were apparent.

By the early 1960's three powerful movements had emerged. The American civil rights movement, the international nuclear disarmament movement, and the student and youth movement, or new left, which also cut across national boundaries. All of these movements influenced each other and helped to create other movements, filling out the agenda for social and political change. But the imminent danger of a Third World War, a nuclear war, was the single most galvanising force for millions of people. Beginning with mass protests against the testing of atomic bombs — from 1945 to 1962 a total of 423 explosions took place, with the U.S. leading in the number of tests — the movement expanded in scope, going on to oppose the arms race and later to organise against the war in Vietnam and the Soviet invasion of Czechoslovakia. Accompanying the fear of war, which was primary, was the growing fear of the health hazards and damage to the environment attendant upon military research testing and production.

The more radical new left youth in turn began questioning and organising against a political and economic system that did not respond to demands for fundamental change. By the mid-1960's this movement was pounding on the doors of power in almost all industrial countries: the U.S., Britain, Canada, France, Italy, Japan; central European countries such as Czechoslovakia; Mexico; and several Latin American countries. The politics of protest and radical organising were being learned everywhere and quickly. The clarion call was for 'participatory democracy' from the campuses to society at large. The rise of student activism was accompanied by the development of a counter-culture including the back-to-the-land movement which advocated a return to nature in protest against materialist consumerism. Through its questioning of the dominant modes of existence the counter-culture deeply affected attitudes among all strata of the industrial societies. This was also the period when more scientific information on environmental conditions began to be assembled and disseminated more widely and when environmental awareness was accelerated by a series of reported environmental disasters. By the end of the decade the movement against nuclear energy was rolling forward.

The motor force of the environment movement of the 1970s was the battle against the building of nuclear reactors in the United States, Canada, Britain, France, West Germany, among other countries. The ramifications of this burst of construction were obvious; people made the connections between nuclear energy production and the production of nuclear weapons, hazardous wastes, and the potential for accidents with devastating effects, especially on communities located in the vicinity of reactors.

Audiences of up to 10,000 would come out to hear speakers on various aspects of what was happening to nature. And on Earth Day in 1970, the largest demonstration in defense of the environment in history was held in the United States. By 1980, roughly seven percent of the American population, some 17 million people, were estimated to be involved in the movement, and an additional 55 per cent sympathetic to its aims.[8] Ruling elites did not remain blind to the growing public concern and soon enough environmental issues began to make their way into official political discourse. After the Conservative Party victory in Britain, the word 'environment' figured for the first time in the Queen's Speech in July 1970. President Richard Nixon's 1970 Message to Congress declared a new decade of environmental State policy. Thus a new mass movement had pushed its way onto the public scene, placing a new question at the top of the public agenda. And it had at its disposal a growing body of scientific evidence which could not easily be disputed.

In response to grass-roots pressure, the State moved into high gear. The Organisation for Economic Cooperation and Development in Europe reported that whereas from 1956 to 1960 only four environment laws had been passed, there were 10 laws enacted between 1961 and 1965, 18 between 1966 and 1970, and as many as 31 from 1971 to 1975. Environmental programmes and agencies were being created everywhere. The political aim underlying this spurt of official action was to calm the fears of the environmentalists and the concerned public and to confine the issue to manageable proportions. The established political parties expediently refurbished their programmes and rhetoric hoping to capitalize on the popular energy.

The environmental movement was not, of course, all of a piece. One of the largest movements in human history it took root in various countries and drew on diverse political traditions. It was bound therefore to comprise a variety of ideological tendencies. In the following pages we will look briefly at its major components in the North American context. As developments on this continent invariably have an influence on political life around the globe, the North American spectrum finds parallels elsewhere, and especially in Europe.

Conservationism

Before and during the 1960's a number of organisations emerged such as the Nature Conservancy (affiliated to the International Union for the Conservation of Nature) and The Sierra Club, and other similar organisations which were largely composed of people who loved nature and wilderness, such as hunters and campers. They were concerned with preserving 'the great outdoors'. The advocacy of these organisations over the many years of their existence led to the establishment of various national parks as well as State/provincial parks in different parts of North America. These are being preserved by the State as part of a public policy of conserving 'our natural heritage'. Earlier we referred to this lobby as preservationists, but in North America they have become part of the conservationist movement. Conservationism has at least two wings. One seeks to enlighten corporations and believes that environmental problems can be assimilated to the larger problem of the "correct" division of property in society. It is the contention of this school that if all the air, water, and land was privately owned, rights to pollute could then be sold at a market price, perfectly balancing industrial and environmental interests. It has been the policy of political conservationists like Reagan, Bush and Thatcher to sell rights to industry with the belief that market capitalism will regulate all. The other wing, which is represented in the U.S. for instance, by the left-wing of the Democratic Party subscribes to the ideal of liberal democracy and advocates limited State regulation to deal with environmental problems. This branch of conservationism overlaps with the environmentalist current described below.

Environmentalism

The approach of environmentalism is to deal individually with one crisis after another. Environmentalists tend to concentrate on bringing about small but urgent changes to the present order of things. Taken alone, however, these intense but circumscribed efforts tend to draw attention away from the need for changes in society's basic institutions of power. The result is that the larger picture gets lost; the forest cannot be seen for the trees, as it were. The environmentalist school is informed by the tenets of current liberal philosophy, as exemplified by such organisations as the Natural Resources Defence Council, Greenpeace, Friends of the Earth, Pollution Probe, and The Sierra Club. Groups such as these believe in technical solutions to environmental problems and maintain that State policy must be changed to assure the passage of more protective legislation.

Although influenced by conservationism, the environmentalists differ from the conservationists insofar as they are not opposed to and even encourage mass popular action as a means of bringing pressure to bear on the powers that be in support of their goals; they also espouse a wider range of environmental concerns.

Organised primarily at the national level, these groups tend to be highly professionalized, employing well-paid and trained staff, and hierarchical in structure; they rely on the organisational technique of mass mailings to thousands of people simultaneously; and they use refined legal and government/corporate lobbying techniques, instead of being grass-roots democratic membership organisations. They welcome financial contributions without paying too much regard to the source of donations. While most of their positions implicitly challenge the dominance of large corporations, they shy away from any overtly radical criticism of the political and economic system as such, partly in order not to alienate politicians and the corporate elites.

Environmental Populism

There are hundreds of thousands of self-avowed environmentalist groups across North America at the local level. These local groups have in turn exercised a significant influence on the voluntary sector, with the result that thousands of small local actions to improve the environment are taken by community organisations and other local associations ranging from the Boy Scouts to church groups. Local environmental groups usually focus their attention on specific environmental issues. Actions are organised against incineration or landfilling of municipal waste, the effects of acid rain, nuclear power plants, hydro-electric projects, the use of pesticides, and so on. Except for some trade unions which organise around occupational hazards at the workplace, these activists have few financial resources and few paid workers; they are usually community-based and may network with similar groups elsewhere.

While these groups have no defined ideology, they express anti-corporate sentiments, since they often confront profiteering by companies at the expenses of human health and needs. Their militancy is often undercut, however, by their own town's or city's dependence on jobs and taxes from the corporations they are fighting. These activist groups lack a global analysis of the ecology crisis and the need for a radical alternative to present State and corporate policies. They are often motivated by the NIMBY syndrome (not in my back yard). It is these activists who generally support alternative life-styles from health food stores to 'green products', and mobilize around annual Earth Day actions. They display all the right instincts, but rarely do they articulate a serious alternative politics.

Deep Ecology

Turning to the more radical popular responses to the environmental crisis, we find the deep ecologists. In spite of a large body of literature devoted to the theme of deep ecology, this current is difficult to define. It originates with the desire to go beyond conservationism and environmentalism but attempts to do so without articulating a new social and historical project. Often verging on anti-rationalism in its celebration of 'the natural,' it seeks to replace an anthropocentric ethics and politics with what is referred to as biocentrism. In this view, the Earth, personified as Gaia, is intrinsically valuable, that is, its value is not predicated upon its utility for human beings, and all life — animate or inanimate — is equal within nature. Deep ecologists hold that in order to reduce destructive human pressures upon the Earth population growth must diminish. Some deep ecologists have argued that pre-industrial societies lived in harmony with nature and that it is European civilization which has destroyed this relationship of equilibrium. As Michael Tobias has observed,

> Deep Ecology concerns those personal moods, values, aesthetic and philosophical

convictions which serve no necessarily utilitarian, nor rational end. By definition their sole justification rests upon the goodness, balance, truth and beauty of the natural world, and of a human being's biological and psychological need to be fully integrated within it. [9]

There is some overlap between deep ecologists and New Age enthusiasts who are primarily concerned with changes in life-styles, personal change, self-realization and spirituality, rather than social and political change. There is also however the eco-guerilla version of deep ecology called EARTH FIRST! Militants in this organisation believe that most land in the U.S. should be returned to its pristine natural state, and consequently they have engaged in such acts as the sabotage of construction sites and equipment to stop lumber companies, as well as the spiking of trees with steel nails to stop trees from being cut, sometimes imperilling the lives of loggers. Some EARTH FIRST! militants have taken positions with racist implications, such as regarding famine as a 'natural' measure against overpopulation which should not be mitigated by human assistance.

Bio-regionalism

According to the bio-regionalists, the environment should be viewed as a collection of bioregions each possessing its own ecological integrity. All other political divisions such as national borders are considered arbitrary and artificial. In their view, society should be decentralized and all political and economic demarcations should correspond to bioregional boundaries.

Bioregionalism means living within the "limits and the gifts provided by a place, creating a way of life that can be passed on to future generations."[10]

By learning to live within the limits of our own ecological region, we will be able to "grow out" towards a more sustainable world. Kirkpatrick Sale identifies a number of bioregions that take both ecosystems and human communities as their base. He sees these ecosystems as the largest natural divisions since they share a common ecology, such as native vegetation and "soil contours" that could cover thousands of square miles. Such divisions are followed by a georegion that might be a river basin, mountain range or plateau. At the local level, which Sale calls the vitaregion, is where human needs are defined. Accordingly, the vitaregion must of necessity provide for the needs of its inhabitants, as "the most elemental and elegant principle" of the natural world this is what is called "self-sufficiency."

> ... dwellers in the land (should) come to know the earth, fully and honestly, the crucial and only all-encompassing task is to understand the place, the immediate specific place where we live .... We must somehow live as close to it as possible, be in touch with its particular soils, its waters, its winds ....[11]

The human-scale and human-centredness to be found in Sale's thesis that each local area will

sustain the basic needs of people does not logical-
ly follow. There is no apparent reason why a
particular area should meet *all* basic needs. There
are, afterall, many large areas of the Earth where
both climate and geography are not condusive to
self-reliance. How are we to deal with natural
limits of an environment. Not all continents have
the ecology of North America.

What is confused in bioregionalism is the
tendency to equate local democracy and
autonomy with a decentralisation based auto-
matically on ecological sustainablity and self-sufficiency. The application of these two principles
may take different shapes in different regions
depending on size. Bioregionalism assumes that
local awareness of an ecosystem helps human
understanding of the wider or global ecological
context. There is a repetition here of the notion
that the whole is the sum total of its parts common to mechanistic science. This claim is as er-
roneous as that held by Deep Ecology to the
effect that since all things are connected, our
minds are also connected in a similar organic
manner. This spiritual idea, "Being is knowing" is
challenged by those who believe that the ecological basis of human life would need to be understood through a conscious process of learning.
Knowing the specificity of one's own region
would need to be mixed with a local, regional and
global programme for self-conscious *political* action. We need to understand the ecological reality
of the Earth in a social context. Thus it appears
that bioregionalism tends toward New Age cul-

tural perspectives, rejecting social and political activism as a privileged means of effecting desired change. What is refreshing about bioregionalism is its claim that the "natural" boundary of human social organisation need not be the nation-State, or the political borders that have been drawn within States, such as counties, cities, districts. Making the primary place of political decision-making the ecological context within which we live lends our future towards a "natural" internationalism.

Eco-feminism

Eco-feminism has its origins in women's anti-militarism mobilizations. It was defined by the Left Green Network in their manifesto as follows:

> The liberation of women is essential to the creation of a free, peaceful, ecological society. Though capitalism has carried the dehumanization of people and the destruction of nature to new heights, the roots of our social and ecological crisis are older than capitalism. They go back thousands of years to the emergence of patriarchy, and with it, the early militarism of neolithic warrior castes, a turn of history that laid the basis for the male-oriented culture structured around hierarchy, domination and conquest that has poisoned our social development ever since.

> Eco-feminism affirms the historical and life experience of women as nurturing beings with a strong sense of connection to nature that cultural feminism has emphasized, while refusing to accept a biological determinism

that reduces the explanation of male domination to genetics. Eco-feminism also affirms the historical analysis and critique of male domination and material exploitation that socialist feminism has emphasized, while refusing to accept an anti-naturalism that seeks to build a realm of human freedom by denying our connection to nature and regarding non-human nature as existing purely for instrumental human ends. Eco-feminism seeks to draw the best insights of both cultural and socialist feminism into the non-dualistic, holistic view of society and nature (including human nature) that it is has drawn from social ecology.[12]

Since the publication of this articulation of eco-feminism by social ecologists, a variety of eco-feminist schools have emerged. Carolyn Marchant for instance identifies — liberal eco-feminism, cultural eco-feminism , social eco-feminism, and socialist eco-feminism, all of which are variants of the initial formulation.[13]

In her important critique of eco-feminism, *Finding Our Way: Rethinking Eco-Feminist Politics*, Janet Biehl,[14] one of the pioneers of left Green politics in the U.S. turns her back on this form of feminism. To her it has become so heavily influenced by the irrational to the point of embracing goddess worship and witchcraft. Crystals and pentagrams, chanting and drum-beating, rituals and meditations used to raise group consciousness are considered by Janet Biehl and other political ecologists as ineffective in dealing with the ecological crisis. When 'spirituality' becomes a political and organising principle, writes

Janet Biehl, and is presented as a means to improve life it must be examined like any other political programme.

> A critical analysis of goddess worshipping spirituality … must address not only the content of the specific myth being generated, but also the function of the myth in an advanced industrial capitalist society.

Janet Biehl argues that cultural symbols should not be confused with social realities. Symbols are not the same as institutions. A dominant religious authority, even a goddess is not more desirable than a secular society. Much of eco-feminism:

> … biologize (s) and essentialize(s) the caretaking and nurturing traits (of women) … and reject(s) scientific and cultural advances just because they were advocated by men.[15]

Eco-feminism seems to imply that what men do to the environment is evil while what women do is good. The privileged relationship of women to nature and the politics that follow exclude men from developing an ethic of caring for the Earth. Eco-feminism also avoids an analysis of capitalism and why it so dominates nature. It does not face the problem of poverty or racialism experienced by millions of women. What appears to follow is a weak perspective for social and political change.

This ideological map of citizen response to the environmental crisis cannot be completed without a discussion of what is arguably the most coherent and promising current within the ecology movement, political ecology, under which rubric belong the Greens in their eco-Marxist, eco-socialist, and social ecologist manifestations. It is to this task that the following section is devoted.

Notes

1. Gore, Al: *Earth in the Balance*; (New York: Plume/Penguin, 1993). p. 82
2. ibid,. p. 73
3. ibid., p. 156
4. ibid., p. 10
5. Philip Lowe and Jane Gayder, *Environmental Groups in Politics*, (London: George Allen & Unwin, 1983). p. 1
6. ibid.,
7. ibid.,
8. Council on Environmental Quality, *Environmental Quality 1980*, (Washington, D.C.: U.S. Government Printing office, 1980). p. 418-422
9. Tobias, Michael, (ed.), *Deep Ecology*. 1985
10. Plant Judith, "Searching for Common Ground : Ecofeminism and Bioregionalism" in Irene Diamond and Gloria Feman Orenstein (eds.) *Reweaving the World*, San Francisco: Sierra Book Club, 1991). p. 158
11. Sale, Kirkpatrick, "Bioregionalsim" in Andrew Dobson (ed), *The Green Reader*, (London: André Deutsch, 1991). p. 79
12. "Towards a New Politics: Principles and Programme of the Vermont and New Hampshire Greens," (Montréal: *OUR GENERATION*, Volume 20, No. 1, 1988). p. 22-54
13. Marchant, Carolyn, *Radical Ecology*, (New York: Routledge, 1992).
14. Biehl, Janet, *Finding Our Way — Rethinking Eco-Feminist Politics*, (Montréal/New York: Black Rose Books, 1991).
15. Marchant, Carolyn, *Radical Ecology*, (New York: Routledge, 1992). p. 195

Political Ecology
and Social Ecology

SECTION THREE

Political Ecology
and Social Ecology

"The first and most important point to be made about ecologism is that it is not the same as environmentalism. As Jonathan Porritt, current director of Friends of the Earth and the leading speaker for the Green movement in Britain has written,' It seems quite clear that whereas a concern for the environment (a fundamental characteristic of the ideology in its own right) is an essential part of being green,' it is ... by no means the same thing as being green. The principal difference is that ecologism argues that care for the environment presupposes radical changes in our relationship with the natural world and in our mode of social and political life. Environmentalism, on the other hand, takes a managerial approach to environmental problems, secure in the belief that these can be solved without fundamental changes in present values or patterns of production and consumption."[1]

Origins

In the 1960s, a new left emerged which drew inspiration from a new mix of philosophical perspectives. This movement, composed primarily of young people and active on diverse political fronts, gave rise to a number of new social movements by the beginning of the 1970s. As noted earlier these movements included the anti-war, feminist, communitarian, and ecology movements. The basic tenets of belief and methods of action which have characterized these movements up to our own day developed in a fruitful process of cross fertilization which transcended national boundaries. Space limitations do not permit discussion of the numerous theories and analyses of the crisis of our society or the proposed alternatives put forward by these movements. (There is already a considerable descriptive and analytical literature on the origins and nature of the new social movements.) Here, we will simply enumerate some of the principal contributions of political ecology.

Although it is critical of science as traditionally understood, political ecology does affirm that the ecological crisis can be scientifically verified. In contrast with environmentalism, however, political ecology advances the idea that the science of ecology itself cannot be divorced from and indeed imposes certain political conceptions. For example, inasmuch as the ecological crisis affects the Earth as a whole isolated attempts to solve the problem cannot but fail; there must be coordination of efforts, and this on a global scale. However, political ecology privileges action at the local and regional levels against what has been called the "imperialism of the State". In Europe, the Greens advocate the creation of a continent of regions against the preeminence of the nation-State, and call for concrete expressions of solidarity with the peoples of the Southern hemisphere.

Another theme of political ecology is the redefinition of the quality of life in opposition to the ideology of limitless growth and endless accumulation of commodities on which the existing consumer society is founded. A snapshot of a green world view can be developed by contrasting green values and objectives with elements of the prevailing belief system.

1. Capitalist (whether) State or private) industrialism.

2. Predominance of materialist values.
3. Reductionist analysis.

4. A determinist view of the future.
5. Aggressive individualism.

1. A Green/Ecological framework of economic or sustainable development.
2. Search for spiritual values.

3. Attempt at synthesis and organic analysis.
4. Flexibility and emphas on personal autonomy.
5. Toward a communitarn & cooperative society.

6. Anthropocentrism.	6. Biocentric humanism.
7. External motivations.	7. Personal motivation & personal growth.
8. Rationalism.	8. Reason informed by intuition
9. Patriarchal values.	9. Feminist values.
10. Institutionalized violence.	10 Gandhian non-violence.
11. Unlimited economic growth.	11. Quality of life & balanced growth within the limits of nature.
12. Production for unrestricted trade exchange.	12. Useful production of goods & services.
13. Unequal distribution of income.	1 3. Equalizing revenue.
14. World 'free market'.	14. Local production for local needs, self-reliance
15. Stimulating demand rather than consumer protection.	15. Voluntary simplicity.
16. Work for its own sake.	16. Work for its own pleasure.
17. Unconditional acceptance of technological development	17. Social development of science and technology.
18. Centralisation & economies of scale.	18. Decentralisatin & human scale economies
19. Hierarchical social structure.	19. Non-hierarchial social order.
20. Dependence on experts.	20. Participation & consultation of citizens.
21. Representative democracy.	21. Direct democracy.
22. Law and order.	22. Libertarian values.
23. National sovereignty.	23. Internationalism & solidarity.
24. Domination of nature.	24. Cooperation with nature.
25. Environmentalism.	25. Ecology.
26. Management of the environment.	26. Understanding the limits of the ecosystem.
27. Nuclear power.	27. Using renewable energy sources.

28. High energy consumption.	28. Reduction of energy consumption.
29. National security & military production.	29. Disarmament and social & civilian defence.

As noted earlier, the purpose of this book is not to probe the meaning of these concepts. But it is important to note that the range of ideas illustrated in the chart above is integral to the world view advanced by Green parties throughout the world. These ideas evolved in part as a critical response to the limited impact of environmentalism in face of the magnitude of the ecological crisis, as well as in reaction to the failure of Marxism and social democracy to transform society. In addition to introducing genuine programmatic innovations, the Green parties which emerged throughout the world in the course of the 1980's also represented a departure in political style from that of traditional political parties and in their emphasis on grassroots democracy have sought to nourish a new political culture.

The first Green-type political party was founded in New Zealand in 1972 under the name the "Values Party." In 1973, a small political party called "The People" was founded in Britain; it later became the "Ecology Party" and was finally renamed the "Green Party" in 1985. Green political parties have been founded in almost all European countries, and in recent years in central and eastern Europe as well. There are also Green parties in Japan and Mexico. The European parties are linked through an international coordinating body in

Brussels and through the cooperation of 29 Greens elected to the European parliament in Strasbourg. Since the Earth Summit in Rio, Green parties throughout the world have established international connections.

In Canada, there is a small national Green party, and several provincial Green parties. In the U.S. 'The Greens (USA)' have not contested national elections, although a number of state parties do field candidates. Among the Greens on this continent there are those who see the municipality and its neighbourhoods as the exclusive site of political action. They take literally the Green slogan 'think globally, act locally' and view the attempt to create Green Cities as a more historically realistic and desirable project than seeking power at the national level.

Only in those countries which have a political system of proportional representation have the Greens succeeded in entering a national parliament, although elsewhere Greens have been elected to municipal governments and various regional legislatures. It was the rise of *die Grünen* in West Germany and the party's first parliamentary success in 1983 that brought the word 'Green' to world political attention. *Die Grünen* published a far-reaching programme for change which was a synthesis of the most original and creative ideas of the new movements of the 1960s and 1970s. They proposed an integrated approach to the current ecological, economic and political crises, which, they stressed, are inter-related and global.

The Greens are not solely concerned with the environmental crisis, although they address it with urgency. They advocate a multi-issued approach, and promote political action through independent Green parties, in close liaison with various social movements. However, the spectrum of Green views ranges from 'light Greens' (principally reformers who advocate compromise and engaging in electoralism to 'get things changed') to 'dark Greens' (fundamentalists, red Greens, and anarcho-Greens who emphasize grassroots activism — combined with selective electoral participation understood primarily as educational activity — and who synthesize radical politics, feminism and anti-militarism).

One of the main weaknesses not only of the German Greens but of the majority of Green parties is that they have failed to develop a sufficiently profound critique of the limits of liberal democracy and parliamentarism. Consequently they do not possess a radical understanding of the dynamics of State political power and the present system's capacity to co-opt forces of opposition. We will return to this crucial question later on.

The Trajectory of Political Ecology: the Case of the Greens in France

The national milieu or dominant political culture in France is not propitious to the development of autonomous socio-political movements. One of the legacies of Jacobinism has been the diminishment of the sense of individual responsibility and an excessive dependency of citizens on the State which undermines sustained collective action. Civil society is, therefore, relatively weak, and this imposes an extra burden on any political movement that seeks to form partnerships with various citizen associations. The electoral system of the Fifth Republic also poses barriers to new parties, especially at the national level. And the pervasiveness of American culture, particularly in the form of the materialistic individualism of the 1980s, has had a regrettable effect on the popular imagination. Nevertheless, we should not forget that it is in France, and more specifically in Paris, that the new left reached its zenith with the revolutionary general strike of 1968, when 10 million people, mainly students and workers, stepped onto the historical stage.

The struggle to establish ecologism in France — and to establish it independently of the traditional French Left — has been a long and complicated one, especially as the post-1968 libertarian left is moribund and the anarchist left proposes no programme for institutional change short of a revolutionary transformation of the existing social order. Many members of the generation of '68 who have not retreated into private life have joined the Greens. But many more Greens are either political neophytes or basically apolitical beyond expressing a genuine concern with the state of the environment.

The heritage of the May '68 movement was culturally and politically diffuse, finding expression in modern feminism, consumer protection associations, and regionalism. It nevertheless constituted a kind of resistance to the conservative government of Valéry Giscard d'Estaing. The heirs of May 1968 were libertarians who privileged extra-parliamentary action and the politics of the streets over electoralism and working within institutions like political parties. In the 1980's, the principal interest of many of these individuals lay in attempting to create a social alternative in isolation from the dominant society. It was these efforts which eventually lead to the creation of a green party.

As many commentators have observed, the events of May 1968 had a profound impact on environmentalists in France and contributed to raising the general awareness of ecological problems. By 1971, a French section of the Friends of The Earth (*Les Amis de la Terre*) had been founded which was to contribute greatly to the development of political ecology in the years that followed.

The first major environmental contest won in France was the 1969 battle over the building of a winter sports complex in the national park, La Vanoise. Half a million letters of protest and the campaigns of preservationists succeeded in putting a halt to the construction project.

By early 1970, the nuclear energy debate had begun. That same year, some 15,000 people demonstrated in opposition to a planned nuclear power plant at the site in Bugey (Ain). At the same time, the famous battle at Larzac began, a saga in the history of non-violent resistance during which farmers undertook a prolonged campaign against the French military's encroachment on agricultural land. Larzac became a symbol for both ecologists and pacifists. The first major demonstration at Larzac took place in the fall of 1971 and involved 6,000 people including the left socialists and Marxist-Leninists. The struggle against the expanded military base continued for 10 years until the election of President François Mitterand, who cancelled the military's plans. Again in 1970, the ecologists engaged in a new form of protest, using bicycles to oppose the construction of an expressway on the Parisian left bank of the Seine river. The protest resulted in the cancellation of this urban planning project.

The growing ferment of the 1970s gave rise to a plethora of publications dealing with environmental issues, including Jean Dorst's *La Nature dé Naturée*, articles by Pierre Fournier in the satirical magazine *Hara-Kiri Hebdo*, the eco-anarchist journal *La Gueule Ouverte*, J.L. Burgunder's *Agence de Presse Réhabilitation Ecologique*, the journal *Sauvage*, and the writings of Michel Bosquet (André Gorz) in *le Nouvel Observateur*. The writings of Ivan Illich also became influential in France at this time.

During the presidency of Valéry Giscard d'-Estaing, the ecology movement was primarily influenced by the libertarians of 1968 and espoused an extra-parliamentary approach, seeking alternatives to working within established institutions. Although some political ecologists did participate in elections they were inclined to do so solely for educational purposes.

The focal point of the ecologists in France (as elsewhere) was the struggle against the use of nuclear power. The unfolding of this battle in France and the ultimate failure to scuttle the ambitious State programme for the building of nuclear reactors had a decisive influence on the shape of the ecological movement in that country. In 1974, Prime Minister Pierre Messmer launched a State nuclear energy programme (Plan Messmer) which set a national objective of using nuclear energy to generate 70 per cent of all electric power before 1985.

In Brand-St-Louis (Gironde), opposition to a nuclear reactor began to build in 1974, when a coalition of farmers, environmentalists and ecologists gathered a petition of some 26,000 signatures. A national rally took place in August 1975 when the *Electricité de France* building was occupied by farmers and a bomb exploded. Popular resentment erupted as construction of the reactor began before any public consultation were conducted.

Confrontations took place in Flamanville (Manche) between 1974 and 1978, pitting farmers, environmentalists and ecologists against construction workers, municipal councillors and the local priest .

But it was at a mass demonstration in Malville, 31 July 1977, that the anti-nuclear struggle came to a head. The Super-Phénix nuclear reactor had been the object of demonstrations since 1976. A year later this site had become a European symbol and ecologists as well as others on the political Left crossed borders to join the protest. In the clash with the forces of the State several hundred demonstrators were injured, and one, Michel Vitalon, a 33 year old teacher, was killed. The action also gave rise to a conflict between the ecologists and pacifists and the street fighters of the authoritarian Left, especially the Maoists. The latter were determined to precipitate a riot and prompt a confrontation with the police.

Following Malville, a series of further actions were organised, but participation began to decline. In 1979, a series of demonstrations that had begun in 1973 in Golfech (Tarn-et-Garonne) culminated in a local referendum in which 83 per cent of the local population expressed its opposition to the reactor. In Charbourg (Manche) in 1979, demonstrations took place opposing the transportation of nuclear waste from Japan to the Hague for processing. In Graveline (Nord) and Tricastin (Drôme), the first trade union protest took place involving the CFDT and CGT, the two largest unions. In Chooz (Ardennes) in 1979, public hearings were followed by violent demonstrations. In Le Pellerin (Loire-Atlantique), several agricultural communes opposed a projected nuclear reactor. This conflict assumed regional proportions with a parallel struggle occurring in Plogoff (Finistére) involving violent confrontations between villagers and the State police. Plogoff was the site of the last major anti-nuclear battle in 1980 and the only popular victory. Violent clashes with the State authorities escalated, and when Mitterand acceded to State power the Socialists cancelled the construction of the reactor.

After Malville, the opposition did not subside, but it did assume a more local character, although the accident at Three Mile Island temporarily stimulated some interest in national coordination of the anti-nuclear struggle. But all of this protest failed to deter the State from pursuing its nuclear energy programme; indeed, when the Socialist Party took power it decided to proceed with its completion.

The failure of the opposition movement can be explained by factors largely external to the movement itself. The highly centralised State and its extensive nationalist propaganda militated against a legitimate role for civil society and obstructed the politics of pressure groups and public consultation. For instance, in France, public hearings are only held after the State has developed its plans, conveying the distinct impression of a *fait accompli*.

The French State, bearing the stamp of Gaullism, draped the nuclear programme in a nationalist veil. To win public opinion over to the large scale construction of nuclear reactors, it used the rationale of freeing the nation from dependency in matters of foreign policy, military capacity (witness the French stock piling of atomic weapons) and energy. With all the traditional political parties echoing this line the potential for opposition was extremely limited. Although Mitterand had himself signed a popular anti-nuclear petition in 1980, when the Socialist Party took power in May 1981 it simply continued the State's sacrosanct nuclear programme. During the preceding years the anti-nuclear and peace movements were part of the general political opposition to the conservative government and hence the Socialist Party had assimilated as much of the anti-nuclear rhetoric of the 1960's as it could digest. And once in government, the Socialists contributed significantly to the demobilization of the extra-parliamentary opposition, by, for example, co-opting some of the key actors in the protest movements.

The inevitable ideological differences inside the extra-parliamentary opposition, between anarchists and Marxists, pacifists and street fighters, also contributed to the exhaustion of energies. No single tendency was able to assert its dominance and the continuing internal disunity sapped the movement's strength. The mould was cast at Malville: the reformists sought to appeal to the interests of all social classes, the revolutionaries wanted to overthrow the "bourgeois State." This combination of factors isolated and weakened the new social movements of the 1970's.

The ecologists survived this period, however, and with them survived some of the major social and political ideals of the sixties and seventies, including the creation of an alternative society. But ecologists are guided by the idea of a dynamic evolution towards a new social order, in contrast with the old left conception of revolution as a sudden break. And one of the ways in which the ecolgists survived the sectarian battles of the 70's was to create a thriving counter-culture as a kind of prefiguration in the present of the new society they wished to build in the future.

After 1968, there was a flight away from the urban centres, not dissimilar to the back-to-the-land movement of the American counter-culture. Participants in this voluntary exile rejected productionism and sought more convivial inter-personal relations.

During the 1970's, all sorts of agricultural experiments were launched throughout France by disillusioned revolutionaries seeking to build ideal self-managed libertarian communities at a distance from technocratic civilization.

This movement gave form to the idea of resis-tance to the consumer society, and explored the possibilities of alternative agriculture and soft technology, in an attempt to build a new way of life. A cooperative movement was revitalized and an alternative social economy gave rise to *Agence de Liaison pour le Développement d'une Economie Alternative (ALDEA)*, which in turn influenced the creation in West Germany of both the *Netwerk Selbsthilfe* (autonomous mutual aid network) in 1978 and the alternative bank *Ökobank*. These enterprises stress viability, autonomy, self-management and solidarity.

These small-scale radical reforms multiplied and by 1989 there were some 750 alternative agricultural experiments going on, 300 coopera-tives and consumer groups, some 100 associa-tions promoting new energy technologies, in addition to many examples of the self-construction of homes and so on.[2] But to what extent did this constitute a genuine step towards social change? How was this budding alternative economy to interact with the existing larger society?

This experience failed to develop into the transformative force it was hoped it would become in part because the ecologists had a limited understanding of capitalism. The alternative left, those outside of State power (PSU/CFDT), who stressed the anti-capitalist principle of self-management, were more resistant to cooptation than the ecologists, who placed the emphasis on creating an "alternative society" without developing a fundamental critique of capitalism. Hence, by 1986, for example, about 90 per cent of ALDEA's budget depended on State contracts. Many of the organisation's activities paralleled those of the State — a situation which suited the latter perfectly as it facilitated the process of social control and the absorption of oppositional forces into the system.

Until 1984, there was no unified political ecology organisation in France. Participation in elections was episodic and ephemeral. The well-known agronomist René Dumont ran as an ecologist candidate for the presidency in 1974, but only in order to promote public awareness of environmental issues, or so he explained his decision at the time. He succeeded in winning 337,800 votes, 1.3 per cent of the total votes cast. Although it did bring the environmental cause to national attention, this adventure coloured the future political strategy of the political ecologists, propelling them into a debilitating electoralism at the national level.

In March 1977, municipal elections were held. These the ecologists considered particularly important insofar as municipal issues touch citizens at a more immediate level. At that time, Pierre Samuel of *Les Amis de la Terre* contended that the ecologists and the alternative left were close to one another: "The social dynamic in France, in 1977, cannot be reduced to a confrontation between right and left. For some years the ecologists have been fighting shoulder to shoulder with the left — the centrifugal anti-statist, anti-productivist currents, the heirs in great measure of the anarcho-syndicalist tradition, and the PSU, the CFDT, the non-violent movement, the regionalist and autonomist movements, etc. These incarnations of the 'self-management' current are the natural allies of the ecologists."[3] As a consequence of perceived affinities, these two tendencies collaborated closely during these elections, with the result that the ecologists captured 9 per cent of the vote, which translated into the election of about 100 people.

These electoral results gave rise to discussion about the possible formation of a national organisation — an idea which was immediately met with firm resistance from some currents within the political ecology movement as it evoked images of a centralised and hierarchically structured organisation. This resistance can only be understood in the context of the political history of France.

Few political cultures outside France have such deeply rooted, though now mostly buried, traditions of revolutionary politics. Within the French left there were and are two streams that have continuously clashed. The first is that of State Socialism whose advocates include Babeuf, Saint-Simon, and Blanqui — who propounded socialism from above by means of a centralised State. This perspective heavily influenced Guesde, Lafargue, and Engels, who in turn assigned to the authoritarian political party the role of subordinating all workers organisations and trade unions. The twentieth century incarnation of this tradition was, of course, Lenin and his Bolshevik vanguard party.

The other stream of socialism was the libertarian tradition which favoured self-management. Proponents of this vision rejected the idea that a new society could be founded through the conquest of State power and argued instead for the creation of socialism from below, through workers associations of various kinds.

In this perspective, smaller communities evolve alternative values and practices which can gradually become generalized, effecting a qualitative transformation of society as a whole. In addition to the utopian socialist Charles Fourier, one of the most notable early exponents of this theory was the anarchist philosopher Pierre Joseph Proudhon; he was hostile to all State authority and to the delegation of power, and he advocated the decomposition of the State in favour of self-reliance, decentralisation, credit unions, and autonomous communes linked in a federation and practising the free exchange of services. (One of the most insightful and systematic of the twentieth century inheritors of this tradition was the Dutch council communist Pannekoek, who argued against Lenin in defense of workers councils and against political parties.)

These two conflicting traditions parted company irrevocably by the end of the nineteenth century. State socialism finally triumphed in our century by becoming a political force of world historical proportions. Although the programme and rhetoric of the French Socialist Party of the 1970's expressed a commitment to "change life",[4] the party sought to accomplish this goal by "changing the State."

The libertarian stream for its part was reinvigorated in the form of the growing ecology movement. The self-management tradition also underwent something of a revival at the hands of some French intellectuals who began to assert the claims of civil society against the State. Moreover, the ecological movement embodied to a large extent the heritage of the libertarian stream of socialism and thus many participants were determined to stay away from traditional politics. These ecologists sought to transform the social order by strengthening civil society through collective mobilisation and by weakening the tentacular grip of government; they envisioned and worked towards the development of direct democracy by promoting citizen action at the local level.[5] " ... [T]he ecologists want to reinvent politics ... the power of the nation-state is not to be taken but destroyed without violence ... the error of the opposition is to direct themselves to central power ... [we invite] people to organise themselves without waiting to be told what to do, to define their own forms of development and the nature of their needs. Ecologists are autonomous. Rather than taking State power, ecologists prefer individual commitment ... "[6]

This rejection of the State implied the refusal of any mediating delegation of power and of political professionalism. These basic convictions found expression time and again in the various publications of the *Mouvement écologique*. In 1976, Françoise d'Eaubonne, founder of the association *Écologie et feminisme*, spoke out against any participation in the following year's municipal elections. In a similar spirit, Roger Fischer observed in a 1977 issue of *'Action écologique'*, a publication of the *Mouvement d'écologie politique* (MEP): " ... [W]hat would it mean for ecology to be committed to a pursuit of central power, to have elected deputies (even if they opposed everything, for how long?) or ministers? How can we pretend to reconcile the irreconcilable, that is, the idea of an ecology of self-management and decentralisation and the game of centralisation and the hierarchy of power." In 1981, Yves Cochet, then member of *Les Amis de la Terre* wrote, "Our vocation is not the global management of society. We do not want to take power as it exists ... our anti-technocratic struggle aims to suppress the means of power." A year later, Michel Carré of the *Confédération écologiste* wrote: "Ecology is the power of the people and not a power facing other powers."

If many ecologists had a deep antipathy to the goal and methods of capturing State power, they were more sympathetic to direct action against an intractable State. On May 3, 1975, the nuclear reactor being built at Fessenhein was the target of a bombing. The press release issued by the Ping Antich-Ulrike Meinhof brigade declared that "eco-sabotage has begun". *Les Amis de la Terre* and the *Mouvement écologique* expressed their solidarity with those responsible. Among these groups, the idea of direct action with its "eco-guerillas", "occupation of construction sites", "perpetual insurrection", and "eco-sabotage" became fashionable. With the rejection of more traditional forms of political action, direct action appeared to many as the only alternative. It was argued also that only a commitment to direct action would prevent ecologists from opting for electoralism.

The fact of the matter was, however, that ecologists had been quietly testing the electoral waters in France since 1974. They had not entered the electoral arena with the aim of taking power, but for primarily educational purposes, to communicate their message to a broad public. It was argued that one of the specific tasks of the ecology movement was to force other political organisations to integrate some green objectives into their programmes. In 1977, André Gorz, writing under the name Michel Bosquet, asserted, " ... the ecology movement can only be a pressure force to help the evolution of the political left and this includes fielding candidates in elections in order to force the debate."

This and similar statements made it clear that political power was not the motive behind the participation of the ecologists in electoral contests. Even when they began to mount serious campaigns at the local level — a strategy which had earlier been rejected — the basic orientation remained unchanged. The elected local councillors were to serve primarily to create links between the Greens and local struggles and to publicize ecological themes. Far from engaging in a discourse of power, the ecology movement strove to maintain pressure on the decision-makers. This perspective was maintained until 1986.

Even this kind of limited political participation was antithetical to some, and met with opposition particularly from militants in the anti-nuclear movement. As Pierre Radanne noted: "[The] anarcho-syndicalist tradition has freguently resurfaced in France — the revolution of 1848, the Paris Commune of 1871, the strikes and workers occupation of 1936, and the events of May 1968 are the products of this tradition. The anti-nuclear movement by its rejection of political parties and established institutions as the radius vector of protest and struggle, is the modern inheritor of this tradition".[7] But in their unbending commitment to non-participation these militants failed to address a critical question: given a social and political conjuncture which is hardly propitious to revolution, is there an alternative both to direct action, on the one hand, and a politics that focuses on national or regional elections, on the other?

After the Socialist victory many people adopted the predictable attitude that it would be worthwhile to give the new government a chance to demonstrate its intentions. During this period of grace the ecology question was largely eclipsed, but in December 1981 a new organisation was founded along Girondin lines, in contrast to the Jacobin orientation of MEP. The *Confédération Écologiste* united the activists of *Aujourd'hui l'écologie, Les Amis de la Terre* and a number of regional organisations. Within a year MEP founded a political party *Verts-Parti Écologiste* and in May 1983 its rival did likewise, founding *Les Verts-Confédération Écologiste*, which, after a congress in Besançon, became simply *Les Verts*.

As these events were taking place in France, the West German Greens made a significant breakthrough, electing 27 representatives to the Bundestag in March 1983. In the long run, this was to have unhappy consequences for emerging Green politics everywhere. Impressed by the success of *die Grünen*, many Greens turned their attention for the next decade to entering national parliaments. But there was also much to be learned from the German experience.

The German Greens had grown out of a broad popular base in the vibrant West German social movements. Inspired by the "German model," the French Greens also attempted to create the broadest social movement base in 1985 in the form of a rainbow coalition which would bring together groups working for community democracy, ecology, feminism, youth liberation, self-management, the rights of immigrants, and Third World solidarity. This attempt was repeated again in 1987. "Let us found a social ecology movement in France. This will take time even though we have the success of the German Greens before our eyes."[8] In spite of much good will and energy, the transition from theory to practice was impeded by numerous obstacles, consisting less in political than in organisational and personality conflicts. But efforts persisted for three years, and a rainbow coalition was actually forged, although it lasted for only 15 months.

Within the Greens a delicate balance was eventually struck between environmental and social issues, embodied in the politics of Antoine Waechter and Yves Cochet. (This attempt at synthesis distinguished the political ecologists from the traditional left-wing forces in France who were largely uninterested in ecological questions at the time.) As the Greens became better organised, however, the national citizens' organisations, fearing they might lose their base of support and funding to a dynamic political party, began to take their distance from *Les Verts*. It was partly for this reason that an effective coalition could not be formed at the national level. Thus in part *Les Verts* built on their strongholds and remained regionally focused and politically decentralised. The regional elections of 1988 showed that the Greens were gaining recognition, although no one was elected. And the municipal elections of 1989 confirmed support for the Greens among progressive people, especially in towns with populations exceeding 30,000. There was a 45 per cent increase in support and 1,369 local councillors were elected across the country. To date, the election results at the municipal and regional levels have clearly been better than the results obtained at the national level, but the political implications of this went unheeded then as now. Local and regional elections are viewed largely as stepping stones to the national assembly. But subsequent experience has shown that the overweening preoccupation with making gains at the national level has not only yielded poor results but has also distracted the Greens from consolidating their growing popularity at the local and regional levels. Furthermore, the basis of a countervailing political theory and practice indeed a dual power has been laid, except that it goes largely unnoticed.

During the period from 1988 to 1992, a former high profile activist with *Les Amis de la Terre*, Brice Lalonde, agreed to accept an appointment as Minister of the Environment in the Socialsit cabinet of the left-leaning Michel Rocard. A scarcely concealed antipathy developed between Lalonde and the Greens, to the degree that in 1990 Lalonde decided to found a new environmentalist political party, *Génération Écologie*. Lalonde sought support for this initiative from other political parties, maintaining that this new formation was not a political party but rather a "movement of ideas and ambitious actions."

With the decline of support for the Socialists, the pre-election polls in the Spring of 1993 boded well for the Greens. Other political parties on the Left and the Right encouraged a wholesale variety of 'independent' candidates to run under one or another "environmentalist" or "ecologist" labels, thus deliberately causing considerable confusion among the electors. However, in spite of the conclusion of an electoral agreement between *Les Verts* and *Génération Écologie* designed to prevent a split in the Green vote, neither party succeeded in electing a single member of the National Assembly.

Towards a New Political Culture

Every nation-State has an official national culture that serves as an institutional and psychological force of integration and socialization. It contributes to inculcating individuals with the dominant values and modes of behaviour. However, these dominant values are never accepted by everyone at all times; especially in societies where there is some degree of pluralism, alternative political cultures may emerge, germinating in the margins.

In France, the official culture is shaped by a certain myth and interpretation of the French revolution of 1789-1792. The concept of the nation and the State are totally fused in the French vision of the republic, and the nation thus conceived itself becomes the object of a kind of secular religion. Both the right-wing and most of the left-wing partake in this tradition. The institutionalized left regards the State as *the* instrument with which "to direct society in the best way," to paraphase Marx when he was discussing the Hegelian dialectic.

This Statist perspective traces back to the victory of the Jacobins over the Girondins during the French revolution. Although all modern nation States exibit a pattern of centralisation, France is one society where that this process has been most accentuated. The centralised State created by the Jacobins and consolidated in the Napoleonic period continues to have serious implications for the shape of political culture in France.

The nature of the official culture is such as to reduce the natural capacity of citizens to assume responsiblity, thus weakening civil society. Of course, France has a strong revolutionary tradition. But because political change has tended to come about through revolutionary upheaval, both the left and the right concentrate on taking power at the centre, in Paris, and the adoption of this strategy by all political parties reinforces the prevailing process of socialisation. It would seem, in fact, that French citizens are inclined to be more politically passive in non-revolutionary periods than their counterparts in other Western countries.

Comparative analysis is revealing here: fewer people are involved, for instance, in environment organisations in France than in Britain or the U.S. This official culture is a particular impediment to the ecologists who seek to encourage public involvement on the part of citizens. It is to their credit that the newly formed Greens — themselves in part a product of the revolutionary ferment of May '68 — have not disintergrated in frustration and disillusionment. Given that they are chronically short of funds and count only 5,000 members nationwide, their influence on the political scene is extraordinary.

In face of the dominant traditions, the political ecologists viewed it as incumbent upon themselves to attempt to forge a new political culture. The ecologists have thus fashioned their own myths, symbols, political and cultural practices — in brief, an autonomous identity. Whether this oppositional culture can withstand the pressures of cooptation remains to be seen.

As noted earlier, one of the founding myths of the French republic is that of the nation of free citizens, equal and fraternal, which is seen as synonymous with the State. The State portrays itself as *the* protector of the people. The ecologists however regard this myth as obsolete and destructive and put forward an alternative vision. They maintain that power should reside in citizen control at the local level, and thus the region, town or village becomes the chosen locus of political action. At the same time, they see the planet as a whole, rather than the nation-State alone, as the ultimate object of social and political transformation. Hence, the dictum "think globally, act locally." This alternative vision of political struggle is coupled with a preference for small-scale economic development, drawing on the "small is beautiful" principle, first expressed by

Fritz Schumacher. Thus, ecologists resist technocratic solutions and mammoth projects. They are suspicious of anything that exceeds the human scale. The reasons for the insistent Green concern with scale have been amplified by Jonathon Porritt who writes:

" ... as we approach various environmental and biological constraints on growth, so we are reaching certain institutional limits imposed by the growing incompetence and declining performance of our bureaucracies. The levels of interdependence and complexity are now so great in many bureaucracies that even the ablest of decision-makers within them are quite overwhelmed. The costs of coordinating this complexity are considerable. The larger an organization or bureaucracy becomes the more rigid and inflexible is it, and so much the less scope is there for creativity and divergent thinking. Similarly, the larger it becomes, the more likely is it that standardized, depersonalized methods of operation will increase the amount of alienation people feel."[9]

Of course, as Porritt observes, the concept of the human scale is more complex than a simple allergy to bigness. Size must be considered in qualitative and not solely quantitative terms. He suggests that what is "too big" is "[w]hatever size it is that takes away our dignity, makes us passive recipients rather than active participants, makes us dependent rather than self-reliant, alienates us from the work we do and the people we live with... "[10]

Alongside their anti-technocratic outlook the Greens express a real commitment to creating, or rather re-creating, community. In 1986, for instance, the current leader of the French Greens stated: "The commune, in particular the small rural commune, is the preferred base for the kind of society we wish. It would be a serious mistake to neglect this."

Not surprisingly the colours green and yellow are used widely in the symbolism of ecologists, the former evoking vegetation and the latter the sun. The sunflower, a popular symbol, embodies both colours, and turns towards the sun, the source of renewable energy. The bicycle is another important icon as bicycle transportation is regarded as one of the means to re-humanise society.

In contradistinction with the tendencies of traditional politics, Green politics demonstrate a keen concern with personal and social ethics, although the party is by no means considered the sole arbiter of moral conduct and much weight is given to individual conscience. For their attention to ethics, the Greens are often rewarded with derision, accused of sanctimonious exhortation and failing to grasp the necessities of *realpolitik*.

The emphasis on individual responsibility also finds expression in the Greens' democratic decision-making structures. From their beginnings in the *Mouvement Écologique* in 1974 until the formation of a political party ten years later, *Les Verts* took great pains to establish what they now consider genuine and viable democratic structures. One particularly notable innovation was the *Conseil National Inter-Regional* (CNIR), which is the Greens' main decision-making body between membership congresses. The CNIR has 75 per cent of its members elected by regional federations and 25 per cent by the annual congress. In turn, it elects the *Collège Exécutif* with its four spokespersons.

On the request of as little as ten per cent of the membership, an internal referendum must be called. This is a principle the Greens hope to extend to society at large. The Greens have adopted a strict rotation rule requiring those Greens who are elected to various posts to step down in mid-term and cede their places to other Greens. The first practical application of this principle of rotation occurred in 1991 when the members of the European Parliament in Strasbourg stepped down in mid-term. The principle of "primaries" is also enforced; it ensures that individuals elected to official positions within the party are given preference in the nominating conventions held to select the candidates to stand for local, regional and national elections. And in a country where official poltical life is dominated by men, the Greens insist on parity between women and men in all functions. This principle is actually applied more rigorously by the French Greens than by their counterparts in Germany. The developing political culture among the Greens is very much informed by the idea that "the personal is political": that what are usually regarded by the larger society as private matters have a political dimension and that political change begins quite literally at home.

The Greens depart significantly from the traditional left also in their commitment to political independence and autonomy. *Les Verts* never form alliances to support the 'lesser of the evils' in the second round of voting during elections. But not only do the Greens consider themselves different from the traditional left; they also see themselves as distinct from the alternative left insofar as they subscribe to a more comprehensive socio-political vision involving personal as well as social transformation.

The vision of the French Greens encompasses in one form or another many of the central ideas constituting political ecology. In fact, it would not be too much of an exaggeration to say that the brand of political ecology which has been developed in France is among the most complete and systematic expressions of the new radical ecological worldview. One of the reasons for this auspicious evolution is that the political traditions of the left generally have endured better in France than elsewhere. Drawing on those radical traditions, French Greens tend to have a deeper theoretical understanding of the dynamics of capitalism than their counterparts, say, in North America. They have also demonstrated a keener awareness of the dangers of cooptation, than, for example, the German Greens, perhaps partly as a result of the still vivid experience of the French Socialist party in power. Having looked at a case of political ecology in practice, let us turn to some of the diverse currents which have shaped its development.

Eco-socialism

There are many varieties of eco-socialism, into which category fall the eco-social democrats, who seek to blend environmentalism and democratic socialism. All social democratic political parties, inculding the Democratic Socialists of America and the New Democratic Party in Canada, are attempting to integrate environmental concerns into their programmes. However, the programmes of these parties are anchored in the metaphysic of the State, and consequently they maintain that a necessary condition for environmental protection is the election of social democrats to central political power. One of the ways they attempt to legitimize this claim and gain credibility as spokespersons for the environment is by pointing to environmental legislation that has been enacted in social-democratic countries such as Sweden. They also seek to strengthen international bodies like the United Nations, and support foreign aid for developing countries, as in the case of the North-South Commission headed by Willy Brandt (1980) and the Brundtland Report, *Our Common Future* (1987).

Included under the rubric of eco-socialism is the eco-Marxist attempt to synthesize Marxism and ecology. Remaining within a broadly conceived Marxist theoretical framework, eco-Marxists continue to focus on political economy. While taking their distance from Marxist theories which assume the limitless abundance of nature and celebrate productivism and attempting to move beyond reductionist analyses of the primacy of the economic, the eco-Marxists are still inclined to regard change at the point of production as the motor of all social and political change.

In their analysis of the lamentable environmental record of the former socialist bloc, the eco-Marxists ascribe the blame to Taylorism and the wholesale importation of the Fordist model of industrial organisation.

Eco-Marxists remain uncomfortable with the dominant Green accent on decentralisation and the local as the locus of political action and social development. A prominent example of eco-Marxist theorizing is the American journal, *Capitalism, Nature, Socialism,* under the editorship of James O'Connor. In an essay entitled "Socialism and Ecology" O'Connor objects to the Green emphasis on localism, arguing that "most ecological problems and the economic problems which are both cause and effect of the ecological problems cannot be solved locally."[11] Acknowledging that centralism as traditionally conceived by the Marxist left has failed, he calls for the sublation of centralism and localism. He suggests that the only potentially viable form of political organisation is a democratic State but he fails to offer any indications of what concrete form such a democratised State might take.

The majority of the more traditional Marxists, for their part, remain ambivalent toward environmental and ecology movements, seeing in them a tendency to divert attention from more fundamental class issues.

By far the most sophisticated and interesting group in the eco-socialist category are the European libertarian eco-socialists, among whom are the authors of the eco-socialist manifesto *Europe's Green Alternative*. They envision a continent of autonomous regions, rather than nation-States, which are economically decentralised, shaped by feminist principles and built upon social structures which are not based on the arbitrary exercise of power. They maintain that eco-socialist change cannot be brought about by the State and they advocate citizen control of the economy. Their manifesto is worth quoting from at length. In their view the ecological movement is part of a slowly rising wave of international resistance which is "gradually eroding away all authority: employers, technocracy, patriarchy, the military, political parties, the church, the state."[12]

In a section of the manifesto sub-titled *let the State wither away*, they declare:

> "Many of the problems faced by societies can only be solved if the following two conditions are fulfilled: Firstly, the vast majority of people -in theory, all of them- must have a real possibility of defining their own needs and the responses to them, and of controlling the process from beginning to end; and secondly, that the solution should be looked for at a local and regional level, firmly rooted in grass-roots experience which, thanks to the democratic and critical use of new information and com-

munications technology, would be directly linked (with no short-circuits) to global facts. A political reaction to ecological and social risks must, above all, be democratic, decentralised and participative, and as direct as possible. The greater the awareness of the interdependence of life and ecological and social problems, the greater the need for a right to diversity." (p. 41)

How do they conceive of decentralisation?

"Neither feudal fragmentation, nor unification at the top only; a Europe made up of regions does not only mean not creating an authoritarian super-state, but also not replacing the current EC member states by a mosaic of smaller sovereign states. Under no condition may the totally free expression and self-determination of all the federated communities, and the people who make them up, be destroyed. ...

What is required is not destruction, but construction; not to conquer the state, but to create and experiment continually with radically new political institutions. Never before has a solution of this type been put in place on such a large scale." (p.42-43)

From the chapter *What can we do?*, we gain an idea of what the re-definition of citizenship could mean:

"Our eco-socialist project must take into account [the] contradiction between a representative State and direct democracy. To transcend it means both changing the existing State institutions and apparatus (including political parties), and at the same time increasing direct democracy at all levels, in ways as yet unimagined. Each situation will require all the issues to be set out and examined. We will fight all attempts to make poltics into a profession."

Concerned with the dangers of the iron rule of oligarchy, professionalisation and cooptation, they remain wary of political parties as the exclusive form of political organisation:

"As eco-socialists we want alternative, independent, green movements to grow in strength, to respond to innovation and to create as yet undiscovered types of political organisations. We, therefore, hope that the green dynamic does not get suffocated by party politics. Organising as a party is only acceptable as a temporary compromise, in order to keep one's independence and to be able to take part in political institutions. Women must have equal representation. Dissenting views must be expressed and accepted. Responsibilities must be shared, rotated and kept in check. No line, group or person must be able to impose their will over all others; however, individuality must not drown in mediocrity and stereotypes. (p. 94)

In many of their declarations and proposals these libertarian eco-socialists display an affinity with the current of thought known as social ecology, which we discuss below. They stop short, however, of embracing the municipalist approach to ecological and social change integral to the school of social ecology. Although the libertarian eco-socialists in Europe reject the nation-State in favour of a continent of regions, they fail to identify a specific configuration of political and economic institutions as the potential foundation for the radical social and political changes they set as their goal.

Social Ecology

Social ecology is rooted in a rich philosophical framework which is reflected in its politics. Comprehensive and systematic, it represents the greatest advance in twentieth century eco-philosophy. The progenitor of the theory of social ecology is the American radical ecologist Murray Bookchin. Over the last 35 years he has laboured brilliantly to lay the foundation of this philosophy in which history, technology and urbanism are interwoven.

Bookchin has striven to elaborate a non-dualistic conception of the realtions between human society and nature, which can provide the basis for a "genuinely objective ethics." "It is eminently *natural*," he writes, " for humanity to create a second nature from its evolution in first nature." [13] This second nature, Bookchin explains, consists in "humanity's development of a uniquely human culture, a wide variety of institutionalized human communities, an effective human technics, a richly symbolic language, and a carefully managed source of nutriment." This second nature is not an foreign graft on biological first nature, but a result of first nature's own evolutionary processes. Thus, first and second nature do not exist in isolation from one another but in an organic relation which enriches both and in which biological reality is reworked in a dialectical process into social reality. The problem, as he sees it, is that social evolution began in the course of human history to assume a distorted character, moving away from organic cooperative forms of social organisation. What is required in face of the ecological crisis is not a (in any case impossible) return to first nature but a radical integration of the two natures on the basis of the development of eco-communities.

Social ecologists see in these ideas the basis of a new politics, a politics which eschews reliance on the State in favour of the empowerment of communities. In social ecology the municipality is theorized as the natural locus of social, political and environmental change and the neighbourhood, the city or town, are conceived as *the* base for a new democratic politics. As Bookchin explains its:

> "The municipality ... is the most immediate political arena of the individual, the world that is literally a doorstep beyond the privacy of the family and the intimacy of personal friendships. In that primary political arena, where politics should be conceived in the Hellenic sense of literally managing the polis or community, the individual can be transformed from a mere person into an active citizen, from a private being into a public being. Given this crucial arena that literally renders the citizen a functional being who can participate directly in the future of society, we are dealing with a level of human interaction that is more basic (apart from the family itself) than any level that is expressed in representative forms of governance, where collec-

tive power is literally transmuted into power embodied by one or a few individuals. The municipality is thus the most authentic arena of public life, however much it may have been distorted over the course of history."[14]

This is the basis of the commitment of political ecologists or the Greens to decentralisation, self-reliance and localism. Unlike eco-socialism even of the libertarian variety, social ecology spells out and grounds an effective and comprehensive alternative form of administration that challenges the central State in every way. The social ecologists are in fact the only Greens who fill this theoretical lacuna.

Conceiving the municipality as "the most authentic arena of public life," it follows for social ecologists that Green electoral activity should be confined to participation in municipal municipal elections, rather than aspiring to so-called "higher levels of government." As Bookchin suggests, it is qualitatively different for Greens to run a candidate for mayor on a libertarian municipalist platform than for them to participate in elections at other levels of government even as a forum in which to advance libertarian municipalist ideas. One cannot, he argues, divorce the office from its context and make an abstraction of it. The powers of a mayor are substantively different from the powers of, say, a state governor or a provincial premier; they are subject to greater public scrutiny and control.[15]

Confined to the municipal level, electoral participation must involve promoting a radical programme for the decentralisation of power from the "higher levels" of the central State to the municipality, and, further, from the central city council to the neighbourhoods. The social ecologists privilege as a political strategy the creation of neighbourhood councils or assemblies, the forms of which depend on the size of the city. The process of municipal decentralisation would not only re-structure city council to create an assembly of mandated and revocable delegates from the neighbourhood councils; the office of the mayor would itself be rendered a largely symbolic position.

Thus, although sanctioning a limited form of electoral participation, social ecologists remain critics of the existing system of parliamentary democracy. They have drawn the negative lessons of the long and unsuccessful history of socialist attempts to use the parliamentary system to their own ends, attempts which have usually ended in their becoming caught up in the narrow logic of the parliamentary process and in the neutering of radical political programmes. For this reason both the new left and the Greens have tried to enrich existing political democracy with extra parliamentary action and organisation, although it is not clear that this commitment immunizes them from the cooptive pressures of traditional politics. It is precisely this problem that has been the source of some bitter division among the German Greens.

As the prominent American Green Howard Hawkins has argued:

"The Green parties have not made the crucial distinction between *extra*-parliamentary action and an *anti*-parliamentary critique which the anarchists have long emphasized. All the Green parties want to combine extra-parliamentary and direct action. But they have still believed that basic change could be achieved through parliamentary measures. The extra-parliamentary movement would keep their parliamentary representative honest and pressure the State for concessions. The anarchist critique of parliamentary politics emphasizes how the representative republican form of the capitalist State is structured to either co-opt or marginalize genuinely radical parties. The power of the legislature is severely circumscribed by the extra-parliamentary powers of the ruling class residing in private capital and the un-elected bureaucracy and military. In order to be 'realistic' parliamentary players, radical parties must begin to limit their programmatic demands to what is possible legislatively. If they do not accept this co-optation into parliamentary possibilism, they are likely to become marginalized relative to more 'realistic' reform parties."[16]

Social ecology introduces as a programmatic idea the creation of dual power in which official political power is sought but only simultaneously with the creation of decentralised bases of popular control. The strategy is to devolve ever more power to the base in a gradual process of dismantling the central State. Of all the perspectives on power articulated by political ecologists, the social ecologist insistence on dual power is the best grounded historically and philosophical-ly, and thus the most realistic strategy. Hawkins summarizes this perspective succinctly:

> "Despite hundreds of Greens elected into the municipal councils in Europe, no attempt has been made to network those Green elected officials and their organisations horizontally with a view toward building up a growing dual power in *opposition* to the power structures of the corporate State. Instead, success in municipal elections has been merely a stepping stone to the road to 'higher' office. From the confederal municipalist viewpoint, the socially transformative struggle is not between parties competing for State power, but between a popular power based in citizen assemblies and municipal confederations on the one hand, and the centralised State and corporate power on the other."[17]

Decentralisation, self-reliance and local democracy cannot be understood as separate but equally viable options; they are inextricably related in the vision of ecological interdependence advanced in the theory of libertarian or confederal municipalism. As Bookchin writes:

> " ... To be sure, without the institutional structures that cluster around our use of these terms and without taking them in combination with each other, we cannot hope to achieve a free ecologically oriented society ... Decentralism and self-sustainablity must involve a much broader principle of social organization than mere localism. Together with decentralization, approximation to self-sufficiency, humanly scaled communities, ecotechnologies, and the like, there is a

compelling need for democratic and truly communitary forms of inter-dependence — in short, for libertarian forms of confederalism …. What, then, is confederalism? It is above all a network of administrative councils whose members or delegates are elected from popular face-to-face democratic assemblies, in the various villages, towns, and even neighbourhoods of large cities. The members of these confederal councils are strictly mandated, recallable, and responsible to the assemblies that choose them for the purpose of coordinating and administering the policies formulated by the assemblies themselves. Their function is then a purely administrative and practical one, not a policy-making one like the function of representatives in republican system of government." [18]

And he continues:

"Confederalism is thus a way of perpetuating the interdependence that should exist among communities and regions — indeed, it is a way of democratizing that interdependence without surrendering the principle of local control. While a reasonable measure of self-sufficiency is desirable for every locality and region, confederalism is a means for avoiding local parochialism on the one hand and an extravagant national and global division of labor on the other. In short, it is a way in which a community can retain its identity and roundedness while participating in a sharing way with the larger whole that makes up a balanced ecological society ….

Confederalism as a principle of social organisation reaches its fullest development

> when the earning itself is confederalized by placing local farms, factories, and other needed enterprises in local municipal hands — that is, when a community, however larger or small, begins to manage its own economic resources in an interlinked network with other communities. "[19]

The pedigree of this new democratic politics can be traced back to Peter Kropotkin's "Commune of Communes", Martin Buber's "Community of Communities" and the reflections of Paul Goodman. However social ecology has given the concept of direct democracy an ecological, geographic, and political-economic spatial dimension that can serve as the building blocks for a new society.

Social ecology proposes that the way to save the Earth and with it human civilisation is to replace domination, hierarchy *and* exploitation with tolerance of diversity in human culture. This necessitates a richly textured confederation of eco-communities deploying eco-technologies in the quest to restore a balance between humans and nature. The objective of superseding hierarchy presupposes, of course, the systematic extirpation of racism, class society, and the inequality between women and men. In a word, unless society and its major institutions of power are fundamentally changed, we cannot hope to establish that balance with nature which will permit us to reverse the crisis. It is a hopeful sign that social ecology has been gaining ground in the larger ecological movement, renewing the legacy bequeathed by libertarian socialism and anarchism.

It is hoped that confederal municipalist Green political organisations are organised wherever possible with a social ecology informed programme setting in motion the dynamic of dual power. Thus local elections should take on a greater significance.

Notes.

1. Dobson, Andrew, *Green Political Thought*, (London: Unwin Hyman, 1990) p. 13
2. Michaud, Dominique Allan, *L'avenir de la société alternative*, 1989, Paris. L'Harmattan.
3. Vadvot, Claude-Marie, *L'écologie, histoire d'une subversion*. Paris, Syros, 1978.
4. Parti Socialiste, *Changer la vie*, programme de gouvernement du Parti Socialiste, Paris, Flammarion, 1972.
5. See note 10, page 69 of Abéles.
6. Arthur, "Le Pas de Coté écologique," *le Monde*, 3 March, 1978. p. 14
7. Chaps, Tony, "Politics and the perception of risk: a study of the anti-nuclear movement in Britain and France." *West European Politics*, Volume 8, January 1985.
8. Radanne, Pierre, *Pour une fécondation de l'écologie et du social*, text of L'Arc-en-ciel.
9. Porritt, Jonathon, *Seeing Green*, pp.87-88
10. ibid., p.87
11. O'Connor, James, "Socialism and Ecology," *Our Generation* Vol. 22, Nos. 1 & 2 (Fall 1990-Spring 1991), p. 81
12. *Europes Green Alternative-Manifesto for a New World* by Penny Kemp.
13. Bookchin, Murray, "Postscript: "Ecologizing the Dialectic" in *Renewing the Earth*, edited by John Clark, Green Print, London; 1990., p. 202.
14. Bookchin, Murray, "The Meaning of Confederalism," *Our Generation*, Volume 22 , Nos. 1 & 2, p. 98.
15. ibid., p.99.
16. Hawkins, Howard, "Community Control, Workers' Control, and the Cooperative Commonwealth," Society and Nature, Volume 1, No. 3, 1993, p. 195.
17. ibid., p. 196.
18. Bookchin, Murray, "Meaning of Confederalism," p. 95.

19. ibid., pp. 95-96. Space does not permit us to discuss the economic basis of the ecological or Green city, but the analytical literature is growing. See, for instance, the interesting work of Takis Fotopoulos and Howard Hawkins in the journal *Society and Nature* (Volume. 1, Nos. 1, 2 and 3, 1992-1993.

Epilogue

The ecology movement is part of history in the making. Environmental degradation is a highly tangible problem; millions of people can see, smell, taste and hear it. Given the immediacy and magnitude of the problem, it is not surprising that the ecology movement is diverse. It is also unregimented — people move in it, around it and out of it. But it will continue to exist and grow in one form or another. It constitutes an ever present potential, especially insofar as it marks a shift from an overweening emphasis on material values and individual security towards a regard for the quality of life. This is especially significant in the primary polluting engine of the Northern Hemisphere. The traditional models of economic growth, whether capitalist or State socialist, are being fundamentally challenged by political ecologists, as are the dominant values of productivism and consumerism. But there are those creatures in nature which linger fatally in warm water that is slowly coming to a boil. The human species evidences such self-destructive tendencies. Will we make the right choice in time? So far, the action taken has been palliative at best. The political and economic structures of modern States are overgrown and do not respond adequately to organised public pressure. Moreover, the people with the power to effect the sweeping changes necessary to preserving our planet are often beholden to special interests driven above all by the profit motive, regardless of its long-term consequences. Thus, as we have argued, the State management of the ecological crisis has not substantially retarded the pace of environmental destruction, let alone reversed the course towards ecocide. The Earth Summit in Rio (1993) was an instructive illustration of this dead-end.

The choice, therefore, is between the creation of a super world State based on a world capitalist economy that attempts to regulate the environment and minimize the worst impacts of the international war system *or* the programme of political ecology and more specifically the radical philosophy and politics of social ecology which demands the patient renovation and reconstruction of human society.

Listen to the grass growing -think globally, act locally- da capo!

Bibliography

Abélès, Marc. *Le Defi Ecologiste*. Paris: L'Harmattan, 1993.

Aldous, Tony. *Battle for the Environment*. London: Fontana, 1972.

Allan Michaud, Dominique. *L'avenir de la société alternative*. Paris: L'Harmattan, 1989.

Alphandery, Pierre and Pierre Bitoun, Yves Dupont. *L'equivoque écologique*. Paris: La Decouverte, 1991.

Barkun, Michael. *Diasater and the Millanium*. New Haven: Yale University Press, 1974.

Bennahmias, Jean-Luc and Agnès Roche. *Des verts de toutes les couleurs*. Paris: Albin Michel, 1992.

Boardman, Robert. *International Organization and the Conservation of Nature*. Bloomington: Indiana University Press, 1981.

Bookchin, Murray. *Toward an Ecological Society*. Montreal: Black Rose Books, 1981.

Bookchin, Murray. *The Philosophy of Social Ecology*. Montreal: Black Rose Books, 1990.

Bowman, James S. "The Ecology Movement: A Viewpoint". *Internation Journal of Environmental Studies*. 8:2 (1975): 91-97.

Bowman, James S. "The Environmental Movement: An Assessment of Ecological Politics". *Environmental Affairs* 5:4 (1976): 649-667.

Boy, Daniel. L'écologisme en France: évolution et structures" (Atelier: L'Ecologisme politique, constances et differénces au niveau europeen), Paris: *European Consortium for Political Research*, Foundation Nationales des Sciences Politiques, 10-15 April 1989.

Cans, Roger. *Tous Verts*: Paris: Calmann-Levy, 1992.

Chafe, Tony. "The Greens and the municipal election". *Association for the Study of Modern and Contemporary France*, No. 14, May-June, 1983.

Clarke, Robin, and Lloyd Timerlake. *Stockholm Plus Ten*. London: Earthscan, 1982.

Cotgrove, Stephen. *Catastrophe or Cornucopia: The Environment, Politics and Future*. Chichester: John Wiley & Sons, 1982.

Dasmann, Raymond F., J.P. Milton, and P.H. Freeman. *Ecologicial Principles for Economic Development*. London: John Wiley, 1973.

Day, Alan J., and Henry W. Degenhart. *Political Parties of the World*. Detroit: Gale Research Co., 1984.

Doud, Alden L. "International Environmental Developments: Perceptions of Developing and Developed Countries". *Natural Resources Journal* 12 (October 1972): 520-529.

Dumont, René. *L'Utopie ou la mort*. Paris: Seuil, 1973.

Enzensberger, Hans Magnus. "A Critique of Political Ecology" *New Left Review 84*. (March-April 1974): 3-31.

Fox, Stephen. *John Muir and His Legacy: The American Conservatives Movement*. Boston: Little, Brown & Co., 1981.

Golub, Robert and Jo Townsend. "Malthus, Multinationals and the Club of Rome". *Social Studies of Science 7* (1977): 201-222.

Haley, Mary Jean, ed. Open Options: *Open Options: A Guide to Stockholm's Alternative Envirnmental Conferences*. Stockholm: 29 May 1972.

Hardin, Charles M. *"Observations on Enviromental Politics"*. In *Environmental Politics*. ed. Stuart S. Nagel. London: Prager, 1974.

Huth, Hans. *Nature and the American: Three Centuries of Changing Attitutdes*. Berkeley: University of California Press, 1957.

Johnson, Stanley. *The Politics of Environment: The British Experience*. London: Tom Stacey, 1973.

Kropotkin, Peter. *Fields, Factories and Workshops*. Montreal: Black Rose Books, 1993.

Mayer, Sylvie. *Parti pris pour l'écologie*. Paris: Messidor/Editions Sociales, 1990.

Milbrath, Lester W. *Environmentalists: Vanguard for a New Society*. New York: State University of N.Y. Press in Albany, 1984.

Morgan, Robin, and Brian Whitaker. *Rainbow Warrior*. London: Arrow Books, 1986.

National Academy of Sciences. *International Arrangements of International Environmental Co-operation*. Washington, DC: NAS, 1972.

National Parks Service. *First World Conference on National Parks*. Washinton, DC: Department of the Interior, 1962.

Ophuls, William. *Ecology and the Politics of Scarcity*. San Francisco: W.H. Freeman, 1977.

Organization for Economic Cooperation and Development. *The OECD Programme on Long Range Transport of Air Pollutants* (Summary Report). Paris: OECD, 1977.

——————————*The State and the Environment, 1979* Paris: OECD, 1979.

——————————The State of the Environment, 1985. Paris: OECD, 1985.

O'Riordan, Timoth. *Environmentalism*. London: Pion Ltd., 1981.

Papadakis, Elim. "The Green Party in Contempory West German Politics". *Political Quarterly* 54:2 (July-September 1983).

Penick, James. *Progressive Politics and Conservation*. Chicago: University of Chicago Press, 1968.

Petulla, J. M. *American Environmentalism: Values, Tactics, Priorities*. College Station: Texas A&M University Press, 1980.

Porritt, Jonathan. *Seeing Green: The Politics of Ecology Explained*. Oxford: Blackwell, 1984.

Pursell, Carroll, ed. *From Conservation to Ecology: The Development Concern*. New York: Thomas Y. Crowell Co., 1973.

Ridgeway, James. *The Politics of Ecology*. New York: E.P. Dutton, 1970.

Rosenbaum, Walter. *Environmental Politics and Policy.* Washington, D.C.: CQ Press, 1985.

Sandbach, Francis. "The Rise and Fall of the Limits of Growth Debate". *Social Studies of Science* 8:4 (November 1978): 495-520.

Sainteny, Guillaume. *Les Verts.* Paris: P.U.F, 1991.

Schnaiberg, Allen. "Politics, Participation and Pollution: The Environmental Movement." *Cities in Change: Studies in the Urban Condition,* ed. John Walton and Donald E. Carns. Boston: Allen and Bacon Inc., 1977.

Simonnet, Dominique. *L'écologisme.* Paris: P.U.F., 1979.

Stone, Peter. *Did We Save The Planet at Stockholm?* London: Earth Island, 1973.

Touraine, Alain. *La prophétie anti-nucléaire.* Paris: Seuil, 1980.

——————. *The Voice and the Eye - An Analysis of Social Movements.* Cambridge (USA): Cambridge University Press, 1980.

Tozzi, Michel. *Syndicalism et nouveaux mouvements sociaux,* Régionalisme, féminisme et écologie, Lyon: Ed. Ouvrières, 1982.

United Nations Environmental Programme. *Report of the Governing Council of th U.N.E.P.,* Fourth Session, 1976. Nairobi: UNEP, 1976.

————— ————————————. *Register of International Treaties and Other Agreements in the Field of the Environment* (UNEP/GC/INTO/11). Nairobi: UNEP, 1984.

DISSIDENCE
Essays Against the Mainstream
Dimitrios Roussopoulos

This collection, written over twenty years, drives towards the building of the community way of life — a participatory democracy. It reflects conscientious objection, not just to war, but to the whole fabric of a dehumanized society. It stands for civil disobedience, not just of individuals, but, hopefully, by large numbers of alienated people. Most important, this definition of dissent is not intended as a moral gesture only, but as a determined attempt to transform society by abolishing the concentrations of power.

250 pages, index
Paperback ISBN: 1-895431-40-9 $19.95
Hardcover ISBN: 1-895431-41-7 $38.95

THE ECOLOGY OF THE AUTOMOBILE
Peter Freund and George Martin

Considering the widespread impact of the automobile in many contemporary societies, it is surprising how little attention its social and political dimensions receive — even from ecologically oriented thinkers. In this original book, authors Freund and Martin examine the central role that auto production and consumption have played in the 20th century: the overuse and misuse that has caused the major auto markets to be saturated and the costs of auto-centered transport to become prohibitive.

213 pages, index
Paperback ISBN: 1-895431-82-4 $19.95
Hardcover ISBN: 1-895431-83-2 $38.95

THE NATURE OF CO-OPERATION
John G. Craig

The practice of co-operation is full of dilemmas. This book explores these dilemmas between the logic of co-operation and co-operatives, and furnishes illustrations of organizations and movements that have found ways to balance the conflicting tensions. It provides an overview of how co-operative organizations function, how they have evolved, and why they have been very successful in some places and dismal failures in others.

220 pages, index
Paperback ISBN: 1-895431-68-9 $19.95
Hardcover ISBN: 1-895431-69-7 $38.95

ELECTRIC RIVERS
The Story of the James Bay Project
Sean McCutcheon

...a book about how and why the James Bay project is being built, how it works, the consequences its building will have for people and for the environment, and the struggle to stop it...it cuts through the rhetoric so frequently found in the debate.
Canadian Book Review Annual

Electric Rivers *is a welcome contribution to the debate...a good fortune for readers who would like to better understand a story that is destined to dominate the environmental and political agenda in Quebec and Canada for many years to come.*
Globe and Mail

194 pages, maps
Paperback ISBN: 1-895431-18-2 $18.95
Hardcover ISBN: 1-895431-19-0 $37.95

EUROPE'S GREEN ALTERNATIVE
An Ecology Manifesto
Penny Kemp, editor

To meet the challenges of rigorous definition of the nature of society's crisis and the ways that we can begin to emerge from this dangerous period in history, an international group of well-known authors gathered together to produce this exceptional guide through the labyrinth of ideas and social/political action.

200 pages, appendices
Paperback: 1-895431-30-1 $16.95
Hardcover: 1-895431-31-X $35.95

GREEN CITIES
Ecologically Sound Approaches to Urban Space
David Gordon, editor

2nd printing
This anthology presents visions from around the world of an ecological urban model.
...it carves a scholarly depth into the radical changes needed to diffuse our urban crisis.
Montreal Mirror

...the ideas it contains are so sane and sensible that you'll end up wondering why civic politicians and officials have been dragging their heels on green issues for so many years.
Books in Canada
240 pages
Paperback ISBN: 0-921689-54-3 $19.95
Hardcover ISBN: 0-921689-55-1 $39.95

THE NUCLEAR POWER GAME
Ronald Babin

Foreword by Gordon Edwards
A careful and lucid analysis of nuclear power and why it deserves the protest it gets.
Kingston Whig-Standard

A remarkable demonstration of the emergence of technocratic power.
Le Devoir, Montréal
236 pages, bibliography
Paperback ISBN: 0-920057-31-4 $14.95
Hardcover ISBN: 0-920057-30-6 $34.95

ECOLOGY AS POLITICS
André Gorz

translated by Patsy Vigderman and Jonathan Cloud
A fascinating study of the relationship between the ecology movement and political structures.

...rich in ways and means to reinvent the future. A very good book.
City Magazine
215 pages
Paperback ISBN: 0-919618-71-5 $18.95
Hardcover ISBN: 0-919618-72-3 $37.95

Books by
MURRAY BOOKCHIN

URBANIZATION WITHOUT CITIES
The Rise and Decline of Citizenship
revised edition

Bookchin argues for an ecological ethics and citizenry that will restore the balance between city and country.

To reverse the city's dehumanization, social thinker Bookchin here advocates an agenda for participatory democracy...It is significant...
Publisher's Weekly, New York
340 pages, index
Paperback ISBN: 1-895431-00-X $19.95
Hardcover ISBN: 1-895431-01-8 $38.95

THE LIMITS OF THE CITY
2nd revised edition
"City air makes people free." With this mediaeval adage, Bookchin begins a remarkable book on the evolution and dialectics of urbanism. Convincingly, he argues that there was once a human and progressive tradition to urban life which has now reached its "ultimate negation in the modern metropolis."

Valuable for its historical perspective and its discussion of the effects on the individual of the modern city.
The Humanist in Canada
194 pages, index
Paperback ISBN: 0-920057-64-0 $17.95
Hardcover ISBN: 0-920057-34-9 $36.95

THE PHILOSOPHY OF SOCIAL ECOLOGY
Essays On Dialectical Naturalism

Since well before Rachel Carson's early 1960's warning about pesticides, Bookchin's thoughtful critiques of environmental politics have contributed a unique dimension to discussions of society and ecology. In this collection of four essays, he concentrates on the extraordinarily rich and diverse philosophical and theoretical underpinnings of his views on "social ecology."
Canadian Book Review Annual
170 pages
Paperback ISBN: 0-921689-68-3 $18.95
Hardcover ISBN: 0-921689-69-1 $37.95

THE ECOLOGY OF FREEDOM
The Emergence and Dissolution of Hierarchy
revised edition

...a confirmation of his [Bookchin's] status as a penetrating critic not only of the ways in which humankind is destroying itself, but of the ethical imperative to live a better life.
Stanley Aronowitz, The Village Voice

Elegantly written, and recommended for a wide audience.
Library Journal
395 pages, index
Paperback ISBN: 0-921689-72-1 $19.95
Hardcover ISBN: 0-921689-73-X $38.95

REMAKING SOCIETY

Remaking Society provides a clear synthesis of Bookchon's ideas for his faithful readers, and serves as an excellent introduction to anyone new to his work.

...an intellectual tour de force...the first synthesis of the spirit, logics, and goals of the European "Green Movement" available in English.
Choice
208 pages
Paperback ISBN: 0-921689-02-0 $18.95
Hardcover ISBN: 0-921689-03-9 $37.95

DEFENDING THE EARTH
Debate between Murray Bookchin & Dave Foreman
Introduction by David Levine
This book is the outcome of the first public meeting between the 'social ecologists' and the 'deep ecologists'.

...contains eloquent passages by Bookchin, who has a clear and humane sense of human's obligation to fellow human and the natural world...worth reading.
Vermont Times
120 pages, index
Paperback ISBN: 0-921689-88-8 $15.95
Hardcover ISBN: 0-921689-89-6 $34.95

THE MODERN CRISIS
2nd revised edition
The social ecologist and philosopher Murray Bookchin exposes the underpinnings of the arket economy and contrasts its destructive reality with the potential for social and ecological sanity offered by a moral economy.

Bookchin is invigorated by the inadequacies of the old isms...He sketches here a new ism called..."ecological ethics"...which is not based on self-interest.
Kingston Whig-Standard
194 pages
Paperback ISBN: 0-920057-62-4 $18.95
Hardcover ISBN: 0-920057-61-6 $37.95

TOWARD AN ECOLOGICAL SOCIETY
3rd printing
Bookchin is capable of penetrating, finely indignant historical analysis. Here is another stimulating, wide-ranging collection.
In These Times
315 pages
Paperback ISBN: 0-919618-98-7 $18.95
Hardcover ISBN: 0-919618-99-5 $37.95

POST-SCARCITY ANARCHISM
with a new Introduction, 8th printing
This book has energy and command. Its ecological, organizational, and political concerns are ever with us...Bookchin's caustic comments are ever important, rarely finding an equal in the field of contemporary socio-political analysis.
Canadian Book Review Annual
265 pages
Paperback ISBN: 0-920057-39-X $18.95
Hardcover ISBN: 0-920057-41-1 $37.95